taste
a new way to cook

sybil kapoor

taste

a new way to cook

photographs by David Loftus

MITCHELL BEAZLEY

For Raju with love

Taste by Sybil Kapoor

First published in Great Britain in
2003 by Mitchell Beazley,
an imprint of Octopus Publishing Group Ltd,
2–4 Heron Quays, London E14 4JP.
© Octopus Publishing Group Limited 2003
Text © Sybil Kapoor 2003
Photographs © David Loftus 2003

ISBN 1 84000 610 2

A CIP catalogue record for this book is available from the
British Library.

While all reasonable care has been taken during
the preparation of this edition, neither the publisher,
editors nor the authors can accept responsibility for
any consequences arising from the use thereof or
from the information contained therein.

Commissioning Editor   Rebecca Spry
Executive Art Editor   Yasia Williams
Design   Nicky Collings
Photography   David Loftus
Home economy and food styling   Louise Mackaness
Editor   Annie Lee
Proof reader   Nicola Graimes
Production   Keiran Connelly
Index   John Noble
Typeset in Abadi MT and Kabel

Printed and bound by Toppan Printing Company in China

Acknowledgements

Writing a book may be a solitary occupation, but it is
nevertheless dependent on the support of many people
I would like to thank my editor Becca Spry for her unbounded
enthusiasm, Nicky Collings and Yasia Williams for their brilliant
design and Jane Aspden for her support at Mitchell Beazley.
I would also like to thank David Loftus for bringing the book
to life with his stunning photographs, Louise Mackaness,
who styled and cooked all the recipes for the shoot beautifully
and Harriet Docker who made sure that we all had fun. A big
thank you should also go to Rosemary Scoular and Sophie
Laurimore at PFD, as well as to Annie Lee and Nicola Graimes
for their meticulous editorial work and sensible questions.

I would also like to thank Lorna Wing for her sound advice;
Susie Atkins for her help; John Worontschak, wine production
consultant, for his concise information on the nature of
wine; Charles Carey, The Oil Merchant, for his invaluable
knowledge on olive oil; Ian Durrant at Waitrose for finding
Anaheim chillies when none were to be had; and Brindisa for
their delectable salted anchovies. I am very grateful to Wendy
Rahamut, Claudia Roden, Margaret Shaida and Paula Wolfert,
each of whom kindly allowed me to use one their recipes
to illustrate some of the principles in this book. Lastly, but
most importantly, I would like to thank my husband for his
clear insight and constant love.

contents

'I could write a better book of cookery than has ever yet been written; it should be a book upon philosophical principles. Pharmacy is now made much more simple. Cookery may be made so too. A prescription which is now compounded of five ingredients, had formerly fifty in it. So in cookery, if the nature of the ingredients be well known, much fewer will do.' Dr Johnson, from *The Life of Samuel Johnson* by James Boswell, 1791.

This book stems from my obsession with taste – or rather with the five tastes: sour, salt, savoury (commonly called umami), bitter and sweet. They pervade everything we eat, from a tart stick of rhubarb to a savoury (umami) slice of blue cheese. Each one affects our perception of the others, as a squeeze of lime juice on some ripe papaya will quickly prove. The lime's acidity transforms the bland sweetness of the papaya into a sensual piece of fruit that oozes sugary, fresh sweetness. Add a few grains of salt and these tastes are magnified. Cooking is essentially about trying to combine foods whose tastes complement each other. I believe that the key to creating scrumptious food lies in understanding the relationship of the five tastes and their effect upon us. Imagine eating a fried egg without bacon; the egg's allure diminishes without the latter's salt and umami to enhance its subtle natural sweetness. In other words, the most inexperienced cook can create amazing food by applying a few basic rules of taste.

Cooking, like all fashionable pursuits, is often subject to the whims and fancies of chefs and writers alike. Sadly, complex dishes are frequently admired above simple ones. The further dishes are removed from everyday eating, the greater the adulation they seem to receive. They are proffered as difficult or even scientific works of art, whereas in reality there is nothing better than plain, well-prepared food made from the best ingredients.

Ironically, the more our palate is bombarded with tastes, the less we can physically taste. Physiologically, you will appreciate a meal of one or two simple dishes far more than a banquet of carefully contrived, complicated recipes. A plate of smoked salmon, seasoned with lemon, for example, tastes far more intense than an elaborate smoked salmon terrine. And a first course will always seem more interesting than the second if the palette of tastes are very similar.

It is important, however, to clarify what I mean by 'taste'. In the context of this book, 'taste' refers solely to the five tastes that we can detect in specialized taste cells in the mouth. Current research indicates that these tastes are sour, salt, umami, bitter and sweet (umami, has only recently been confirmed as a fifth taste — it is typified by the intense, savoury taste of soy sauce or chicken stock). 'Taste' does not refer to flavour, which is aroma and is picked up by the olfactory cells in the roof of the nasal cavity. Every culinary ingredient has myriad flavours and usually several tastes, each of which vary in strength. A ripe peach, for example, is predominately sweet with a hint of sourness, yet as you bite into its velvet skin, you will taste a little bitterness which is echoed in the flesh that clings to the stone. The peach's flavour lies in the subtle nuances of its scent. Which cook can resist trying to draw out such flattering tastes so that they resonate with one another like a piece of music? Add a few drops of bitter almond essence with some sugar and cream and the peach can be transformed into a sexily bitter-sweet ice cream.

Theories are one thing, and practice another. Having speculated about how taste might work, I decided to test my ideas. The result is this book. Scientists are only just beginning to understand how taste works at a cellular level and many of their findings are hard to relate to everyday cooking, particularly as misconceptions abound as to how we sense taste and smell. Holding your nose while you eat, for example, will not prevent aromas from entering your nasal passages from the mouth. Similarly, the old confusing taste maps of the mouth are wrong when they state that we experience each of the tastes in separate areas of the mouth and tongue. All five can be tasted wherever there are taste cells. Yet everyone has a different sense of taste and smell. Thus, I might find a cube of sugar far sweeter than you do. Even more interesting is the fact that if we eat large quantities of sweet food, we become less and less able to detect sweetness. The same is true with salty food, just as, conversely, the less sugar or salt we eat, the more sensitive we become to their presence. Over-salting also dulls our perception of the four other tastes.

In the interests of research, I discarded my instincts and became a gastronomic guinea pig by sampling such delights as coffee with salt, to see how my perception of the different tastes was altered. Before long, I realized that different combinations of the five tastes not only alter our perception of individual tastes, but also appear to affect our perception of texture and influence our appetite. Sweetened bitterness, such as a sugared espresso, for example, satiates the appetite, while savoury sourness, such as hot and sour soup, can stimulate hunger and highlight texture. The most appetizing combinations of the different tastes all lead towards subtly enhancing natural sweetness and negating any unpleasant aromas or tastes. The best combinations introduce an element of excitement – usually with bitterness or sourness. In essence, the five tastes are like a palette of primary colours which are delicately mixed to accentuate, soften or deepen a dominant taste (colour) in a dish. The aim of this book is to make that selection of tastes instinctive.

It is, however, impossible to consider cooking by taste without examining the impact of flavour. Most flavours colour our impression of the different tastes by enhancing them and adding a vibrant depth. Vanilla, for example, amplifies sweetness in a custard, just as saffron underlines bitterness in a lemon and olive chicken tagine. Chillies have a different role. They contain capsaicin, an odourless, tasteless, irritant alkaloid which has the effect of heightening our sense of taste, flavour and texture. Although many flavours, including chilli, appear in recipes throughout the book, both flavours and chilli have their own chapters at the end.

All you need to enjoy this book is common sense and a love of food. I have tried to write it in such a manner that you can dip into any recipe and immediately understand how the different tastes work together. The principles are easy, and will rapidly become self-evident as you start to focus on the taste of everything you eat, from the bitter sap of lettuce to the umami nature of chicken stock. Everything you consume should be appreciated in much the same way as Alexander Solzhenitsyn describes in 1962 in his novel *One Day in the Life of Ivan Denisovich*: 'More than once during his life in the camps, Shukhov had recalled the way they used to eat in his village: whole saucepans of potatoes, pots of porridge and, in the early days, big chunks of meat. And milk enough to split their guts. That wasn't the way to eat, he learned in camp. You had to eat with all your mind on the food – like now, nibbling the bread bit by bit, working the crumbs up into a paste with your tongue and sucking it into your cheeks. And how good it tasted, that soggy black bread!' Gradually, as each ingredient is explored and understood, you will begin to instinctively combine different tastes to create delicious, simple food.

fundamentals

taste

Whenever we put something into our mouths we automatically note its taste, smell, texture and temperature. Taste is what specialized taste cells in the mouth detect from water-soluble compounds in our food. In other words, as soon as an ingredient comes into contact with our saliva, certain chemicals known as tastants begin to dissolve the food and contact the taste cells through the taste pores. These are located in the taste buds, which are situated predominantly on the tongue and soft palate.

Originally, it was thought that we were sensitive to four tastes, namely sour, salt, bitter and sweet. However, current research suggests that we have a fifth taste, which is normally referred to as 'umami' or 'savoury'. Soy sauce or reduced chicken stock typify this taste. Each taste bud can detect all five tastes, but everyone has a different perception of taste, just as we all have a different sense of colour and smell.

flavour

Unlike taste, flavour is picked up by the olfactory cells in the roof of the nasal cavity, rather than the taste cells in the mouth. These respond to airborne compounds, many of which are released as we chew our food. Therefore, in the interests of clarity, the word 'flavour' will only be used in this book when I refer to aromas that are detected by the olfactory cells. This may sound technical, but in reality, common sense will guide you as all food is a mixture of taste, flavour and texture.

chillies

Chillies have both taste and flavour, but they also contain an odourless, tasteless irritant alkaloid called capsaicin. This heightens our sense of taste, flavour and texture by exciting the palate.

understanding taste

Most ingredients contain several tastes – some, such as tomatoes, have all five. The art of the cook lies in drawing out the most appetizing combinations of such tastes. In order to do this, try to analyze the taste (as opposed to flavour) of everything you eat.

sour

Sourness is found in all acidic ingredients and can vary greatly in its intensity. It is the opposite of sweetness. Malt vinegar is very sour, whereas raspberries are mildly sour as they are also sweet. Sourness imbues food with a delicious freshness which stimulates our desire to eat.

salt

The presence of any salt in food, such as sodium chloride (NaCl), will trigger our perception of it. Most of the salty foods we consume are man-made, but oysters, samphire and seaweed are notable exceptions. The less salt we eat, the more salt we can taste in food.

umami (savoury)

Current research indicates that we possess a fifth taste which is sensitive to glutamate, one of the 20 amino acids that make up the proteins in meat, fish and legumes. Glutamate also serves as a flavour enhancer in the form of the man-made additive monosodium glutamate (MSG) – now widely found in manufactured foods such as salty snacks and stock cubes. The Japanese call this taste umami, derived from the Japanese *umai* meaning 'delicious'. Very little is known about how umami affects the other tastes. It increases salivation and accentuates the savoury, salty and sweet nature of food. Umami occurs naturally in the wide range of foods that contain free glutamate, for example, peas and seaweed.

bitter

Like sourness, bitterness is defined as the opposite of sweetness. Bitterness tastes repulsive unless it is diluted or sweetened. Coffee beans, Angostura bitters and cocoa powder typify bitterness. Cooks should note that bitterness imbues other foods with a sophisticated taste, but an appreciation of this is usually only acquired in adulthood. If combined with sweetness, bitterness appears to satiate the appetite, as can be discovered by eating a chocolate truffle.

sweet

Our taste buds translate both the various types of sugar, such as fructose, glucose and lactose, and unrelated chemicals such as chloroform, saccharin and aspartame, as sweetness. Thus, honey, peas and cream all contain varying degrees of sweetness. Like salt, the more sweetness we consume the less of it we can taste.

temperature

Temperature affects our perception of taste. Tepid food has the maximum taste and flavour, whereas coldness reduces our sensitivity to sour or sweet tastes but increases our perception of salt. Ice-cream, for example, tastes sweeter before it is frozen, just as a hot cucumber soup will seem more salty once it is chilled.

enhancing and negating taste

Cooking by taste is really a question of degree. In the simplest terms, most food has a dominant taste, which is then altered by the addition of another taste. If, for example, you have a sweet taste and season it with a few drops of sourness, it will seem even sweeter. But the more sourness you add, the less sweet it will become until it tastes sour. However, both the sourness and the sweetness will taste amazingly intense unless they are diluted with some form of liquid, such as water, which is why blackcurrant jam tastes so potent.

Thus, a generous dose of sourness, saltiness or bitterness lessens our perception of sweetness, just as sweetness lessens our perception of sourness, saltiness or bitterness, particularly if there is dilution. Imagine tasting the sugary lemon juice of a citron pressé before and after adding water.

Conversely, a small amount of one taste can enhance our perception of the others. A touch of saltiness or sourness, for example, will amplify pure bitterness, just as hint of saltiness or bitterness will intensify pure sourness, as can be discovered by drinking a tequila with lime and salt. Similarly, a touch of sourness, saltiness, umami or bitterness will enhance sweetness. Try eating a sweet vanilla ice cream with and without a drizzle of Angostura bitters. A little saltiness or bitterness will also add an interesting complexity to sweetness by adding a different dimension of taste.

A small amount of umami, sourness or bitterness will highlight saltiness. This would be unpleasant if the salty food contained no natural sweetness. However, since most foods contain more than one taste, the 'seasoning' taste naturally also acts on any other tastes present. A small amount umami, sourness or bitterness, for example, will enhance both the sweetness and saltiness in a salty food. The increased sweetness will partially counterbalance the saltiness. This can be tested by eating some smoked salmon with a little crème fraîche – the fish will seem sweeter.

Similarly, because small amounts of umami, sourness or saltiness enhance sweetness, they will also lessen bitterness in ingredients that contain some sweetness. Season some Belgian endive with lemon juice and/or salt and it will seem sweeter and therefore less bitter.

Culinary techniques to intensify or dilute the individual tastes can be found in the relevant chapters.

sour

Close your eyes for a moment and imagine sucking a lemon. The mere thought of its acid juice spilling over your tongue will make your mouth pucker. This is the first step into a magical world of culinary experimentation; the beginning of understanding the five tastes – sourness, saltiness, umami (see definition on p.11), bitterness and sweetness – and how best to utilize them to create tantalizing dishes. The intense, stimulating nature of sourness can highlight our perception of the four other tastes; it clarifies and defines taste. A squeeze of lime juice on ripe melon, for example, will bring out its sugary freshness, just as a splash of vinegar on chips will emphasize their sweet saltiness. However, in order to understand such dynamics it is helpful to begin by considering sourness itself, as it needs to be handled with discretion to maximize its potential as a refreshing, delicious taste.

Sourness is found in all acidic ingredients, from an unripe plum to vinegar, but it varies greatly in its intensity, malt vinegar being at the opposite end of the scale to a mild crème fraîche. Sourness is defined as the opposite of sweetness, although in reality many sour-tasting foods will also contain some form of sugar, just as they may contain elements of saltiness or bitterness. The skill of the cook lies in recognizing these elements and utilizing or negating them to best effect. Take damsons as an example: in their raw state, they are unpleasantly sour and bitter but, if cooked with enough sugar, their acidity is transformed into a gorgeous vibrant taste, which is deepened and made more alluring by their hint of bitterness. Bizarrely, bitterness is the secret element in cooking; it imbues dishes with a sexy, sophisticated edge.

This may sound complicated, but in reality we all instinctively categorize the predominant taste of our ingredients. A banana is obviously sweet, just as rhubarb is sour and meat is neutral. Any extreme taste is unpalatable, so in the case of a sour food the first step is usually to reduce its acidity by diluting it – for instance, vinegar is often diluted with oil, gooseberries with cream. Then the alchemy of cooking really begins. If you want to intensify sourness and stimulate the palate, the merest hint of bitterness or saltiness will suffice, just as sweetness will negate sourness and ultimately suppress the appetite. In other words, recipes that combine sour with salty or bitter tastes, such as vinaigrette or wine and wild mushroom risotto, make perfect starters and main dishes; whereas a sweetened sour dish, such as sweet and sour chicken or raspberry fool, both stimulate and satisfy the appetite and so are better served as a main course or pudding.

Thus, sourness is the culinary equivalent of the colour white in painting. Even the smallest amount of sourness will add a vibrancy to food by giving a freshness to other tastes, just as a few dots of white will make a painting shimmer with light.

lime

Limes *(Citrus aurantifolia)* have a mere 0.8% sugar in their sour flesh, compared to 3% found in lemons. This intense sourness makes lime a useful seasoner, as only a few drops are necessary to highlight the sweetness in other foods such as seared scallops or roasted peppers. Similarly, lime's sourness can revitalize the taste of other sour ingredients such as raspberries or passion fruit when their sourness has been lessened by sweeter ingredients, such as cream or sugar.

Limes can vary in colour from deep green to golden yellow and, like lemons, have a bitter pith and aromatic skin. Imported limes can lack juice, so buy fruit that feels heavy for its size and roll it under your palm before juicing. Salt, sugar and Angostura bitters are commonly used to alter the taste of lime juice.

tamarind

The seeds of the tamarind tree *(Tamarindus indica)* hang beneath its feathery green leaves in curved, bean-like pods. As they ripen they turn brown and crack open, revealing a sticky, fibrous, dark flesh that is rich in tartaric acid. This is soaked in warm water to extract its delicious fruity-sour pulp. The resulting liquid can be diluted or reduced, depending on your need. Tamarind is often sold in a compressed block, with or without its stones. It can be sold ready-prepared, but this does not taste as good.

Tamarind is a popular souring agent throughout much of the East and the Caribbean. Its acidity can be softened by the inclusion of brown sugar, dates, sultanas, bananas or coconut in both sweet and savoury dishes. If served as a tart, salted and spiced sauce, tamarind will enhance sweeter ingredients such as pulses or fish.

sorrel

There was a time when the astringent leaves of sorrel *(Rumex acetosa)* were loved by cooks. As John Evelyn wrote in 1699 in his book *Acetaria, A Discourse of Sallets*, it imparts so 'grateful a quickness to the rest, as supplies the want of orange, limon and other omphacia (sources of acid taste), and therefore never be excluded'. Gradually, citrus fruits replaced sorrel in popular cooking, despite the fact that both it and the more recently introduced French sorrel *(R. scutatus)* grow like weeds in Britain.

Sorrel's sourness is due to the oxalic acid in its leaves. It is best enjoyed raw in a salad or cooked in a light cream sauce, soup or omelette. But sorrel is also good cooked with other sour ingredients such as cooking apples. Aside from sweet-sour fruit sauces for herring, mackerel or pork, sorrel is excellent in puddings such as apple fritters.

lemon

No doubt, from the moment man or woman first picked a lemon *(Citrus limon)* its juice was used to season food. With a mere 3% of sugar and 5% citric acid, lemon is a gentle but effective source of sourness for everything from raw fish to ripe fruit. Its fruity-sweet undertones bring out the natural sweetness in fruit, vegetables and fish, while its sourness negates any rank bloody tastes in meat and fowl. Even today in the Middle East, raw meat is still rubbed clean with lemon and salt, then rinsed before cooking. If, however, lemon juice is cooked it becomes stronger and more acidic through reduction.

Only the flesh of lemons is sour, their pith and aromatic skin is bitter and should be treated as such. (Aroma, incidentally, is a flavour rather than a taste, although it does affect our perception of taste – see flavour on p.10).

vinegar

In his *Culinary Jottings for Madras* (1885), Colonel A.R. Kenney-Herbert wrote that 'no store-room should be without tarragon vinegar, anchovy vinegar, French vinegar, and white wine vinegar', and, as he adds later, a great many others. Choosing vinegar is a peculiarly personal matter and often reflects the type of food you like to cook. Strong malt vinegar, for example, is excellent on chips whereas mild rice vinegar is better in sushi.

All alcohol will turn into vinegar if it is exposed to air, as it is invaded by aerobic (air-breathing) bacteria that oxidize the alcohol into acetic acid. The finest vinegars are slowly converted and aged, regardless of whether they are made from wine, sherry or cider. Balsamic vinegar, which is made from grape must, falls into the sweet and sour category, so is more useful when both tastes are needed in a dish.

wine

Wine writers may ascribe all manner of sweet nuances to wine, but in literal terms it is an acidic ingredient that contains between 4.5g and 8.5g of acid in every litre, much of which is tartaric and citric acid. Of course, you can buy a bottle of honeyed dessert wine, but this will still contain a high level of acid with the sugar. In other words, wine can be both sweet and sour.

Such acidity makes wine a useful source of sourness in cooking. It can be reduced down to produce an intensely sour, syrupy base to counterbalance the cloying umami nature of a reduced stock, or diluted to stew meat, fish, game, fowl or fruit. In either case, wine's acidity is used to enhance the sweeter tastes of such foods. However, choose your wine carefully, as its quality will be reflected in the final taste of the dish.

yoghurt

Cool, creamy yoghurt lies on the mild side of sour. It is made by converting the sweet lactose in cow's, goat's or sheep's milk into lactic acid by carefully introducing special bacteria – *Streptococcus thermophilus*, *Lactobacillus bulgaricus* and sometimes *Lactobacillus acidophilus*. This process thickens and sours the milk into luscious curds which will vary in sharpness depending on the milk and method of manufacture.

As with all acidic ingredients, you can intensify yoghurt's sourness by adding salt or lemon juice, just as you can deepen its flavour by mixing in a bitter ingredient such as roasted ground cumin seeds, grated cucumber or sautéed aubergine. Naturally, sugar or sweet fruit such as bananas will soften yoghurt's sourness. Yoghurt doesn't lose its acidity when it is cooked.

rhubarb

Technically a vegetable, rhubarb (*Rheum rhabarbarum*) is frequently classified as a fruit because of the Western predilection for cooking its sour stems with sugar. Rhubarb's leaf-stalk contains citric, malic and oxalic acids which can render it as sharp as a lemon. However, Afghani and Iranian cooks have long used this acidity to great effect in savoury dishes, such as stewed spinach with dried dill, or mint and parsley lamb stew. Rhubarb's sourness enhances the taste of other more neutral ingredients such as strawberries.

Rhubarb is sold in two forms: forced and garden. Forced rhubarb is grown indoors in the dark in winter; it has a delicate sharp flavour, fragile flesh and slender pink stems. Garden rhubarb is a summer outdoor plant with greener, coarser, more acidic-tasting stems. In Britain, rhubarb's acidity is usually tempered by sugar, orange juice, cream or custard.

drinks

In writing this book, I decided to throw away my preconceptions about food and explore each taste afresh. According to Harold McGee in his book *On Food and Cooking, The Science and Lore of the Kitchen* (1984), the more familiar we are with a particular taste, the less we are able to perceive it. That's why I decided to begin with the simplest recipes I could concoct, namely drinks, to discover how one taste affects another.

The refreshing nature of sourness makes it a popular taste for cooling drinks, from a luscious iced yoghurt drink to a glass of white wine or a tart cherry cordial. All these drinks need some degree of sweetness and dilution to taste palatable. This may be naturally present, as in the case of wine, or added later, as with a citron pressé, where the drinker seasons his or her lemon juice to taste with sugar and water. Sweetness counteracts rather than dilutes acidity, giving it an amazing intensity.

Salt also changes the dynamics of a sour drink. A small amount of salt intensifies the drink's sourness as well as any inherent sweetness – as can be tested by trying the lassi below. Alternatively, try adding a touch of salt and umami to a drink by mixing celery salt and umami-tasting Worcestershire sauce into tomato juice. Tomatoes may be a mixture of all five tastes, but the resulting combinations will zing around your mouth. Finally, try a little bitterness in a sweet-sour drink; bitterness intensifies the sourness while enhancing sweetness, but it also adds a hint of sophistication, as any gin and tonic drinker will tell you.

lassi

In the interests of research, try this diluted yoghurt drink with and without the salt. Then add either a sprinkling of sliced fresh mint, which will enhance your perception of sweetness, or a few lightly toasted and finely ground cumin seeds, which will add a hint of bitterness, making the salted yoghurt taste sublime.

serves 2

400g (14oz) natural Greek yoghurt, chilled
salt to taste

1 Place the yoghurt in a liquidizer with 200ml (7fl oz) chilled water.

2 Process until frothy, then season to taste with salt and serve chilled.

indian lime pressé

This is a suave Indian equivalent of a sugary citron pressé. Sweetened lime juice is salted and peppered to taste, with the result that the salt emphasizes both its sweetness and sourness, while the pepper (a flavouring) adds a prickly sweet aroma. Try adding salt to other sweet-sour drinks. I have been known to add a pinch of salt to an Orangina!

serves 1

2 limes, juiced
salt and freshly ground black pepper to taste
caster sugar to taste

1 Pour the lime juice into a tumbler with some ice.

2 Add ice cold water, then season to taste with salt, freshly ground black pepper and sugar. Stir and drink.

iced bitter lemon drink

Bitterness adds a sophisticated complexity to sour-sweet drinks, as can be tested here. The Angostura bitters reduces the intense freshness of the sour lemon juice and creates a softer, more intriguing taste which compels the drinker to keep taking another sip. Mint adds a fresh, sweet fragrance.

serves 1

1 lemon, juiced
caster sugar to taste
a few drops of Angostura bitters
fresh mint or lemon verbena sprigs
soda water to taste

1 Pour the lemon juice into a glass. Add 3 teaspoons of caster sugar, a few drops of Angostura bitters, the mint or lemon verbena sprigs and plenty of ice.

2 Stir in the soda water and adjust the sugar and bitters to taste. Serve on a hot summer's day.

soups

Soups often contain a sour ingredient such as soured cream, buttermilk or lime juice, usually added at the last minute to adjust the taste. But some soups are made from an intrinsically sour ingredient, such as yoghurt or sorrel, and these need to be carefully diluted and seasoned to be palatable. In either case, sourness refreshes and stimulates the appetite.

iced cucumber yoghurt soup

Here, cucumber is blanched to make it taste sweeter, while salt emphasizes the yoghurt's acidity and sweetness.

serves 4

4 cucumbers, peeled
3 tablespoons finely sliced fresh mint leaves
500g (1lb 2oz) natural Greek yoghurt
3 fat salad onions, trimmed and finely diced
salt and freshly ground black pepper

1 Cut the cucumbers in half lengthways. Remove and discard their seeds. Roughly slice their flesh and drop into a large pan of boiling unsalted water. Return to the boil and cook for 3 minutes, or until just tender. Drain and purée the cucumber. Transfer to a large bowl.

2 Liquidize the mint leaves with the yoghurt and mix into the cucumber with the salad onions. Season to taste, then cover and chill until needed.

sorrel and lettuce soup

Sour ingredients are often softened by being combined with sweeter foods. Here, the acidity in sorrel is lessened by being puréed with relatively sweet fried onions and potatoes, and umami-tasting stock.

serves 6

2 onions, finely sliced
1 clove of garlic, roughly chopped
4 tablespoons olive oil
600g (1lb 5oz) potatoes, peeled and finely diced
1 litre (1¾ pints) good chicken stock (see p.202)
salt and freshly ground black pepper
85g (3oz) sorrel, leaves and stems separated, both finely sliced
4 little gem lettuces, roughly shredded
285ml (½ pint) crème fraîche

1 Gently fry the onions and garlic in the oil over a low heat until they are soft and golden. Mix in the potatoes and fry for 3 minutes before adding the stock. Season to taste and simmer until the potatoes are soft.

2 Add the sorrel stems to the lettuce. Stir into the soup and simmer for 15 minutes until the sorrel stems and lettuce are very soft. Add the sorrel leaves and cook for a further 2 minutes. Take off the heat, stir in the crème fraîche and immediately liquidize. Season to taste and thin with a little water, if wished. Serve hot, warm or cold.

salads

Having experimented with the pure taste of sourness, it is important to understand how it works with more complicated dishes. The salad is a natural forum for such research, given its sour dressing and disparate taste elements. Consider the dressing. The most basic vinaigrette is one part acid to three parts oil, seasoned with salt and freshly ground black pepper. In other words, vinaigrette is sour, bitter (olive oil) and salty. Its acidity might come from a delicate grapefruit juice, a sweet balsamic vinegar or an intense sherry vinegar. This sourness will bring out any sweetness or sourness in the salad's ingredients, while at the same time lessening their saltiness and bitterness. Thus, a lemon vinaigrette will make pear taste sweeter and sorrel sharper; conversely, it will negate the saltiness of anchovies and the bitterness of olives.

Consequently, it is important to choose an acid that will flatter the salad's ingredients. Citrus juice, for example, will enhance fruit, shellfish and delicate vegetables, while robust vinegars work with stronger-tasting foods such as salty ham, bitter red cabbage or sweet pulses. If you want a touch more bitterness, add mustard or nut oils. If you need sweetness, mix in a little sugar or honey.

prawn, lime and mango salad

Fresh lime juice, rather than vinegar, emphasizes the fruity sweet undertones of the avocados, mangoes and prawns. A few bitter mustard leaves will increase this further. See p.71 for how to clean prawns.

serves 4 as a light lunch

450g (1lb) raw unpeeled king prawn tails
7 tablespoons extra virgin olive oil
4 tablespoons fresh lime juice plus 2 limes, halved
1–2 small red chillies, or to taste, finely diced
salt and freshly ground black pepper
2 small ripe mangoes
1 small red onion, finely sliced
115g (4oz) mixed salad leaves
2 handfuls of fresh coriander leaves
2 small ripe avocados

1 Peel and clean the prawns. Heat a tablespoon of oil in a non-stick frying pan over a high heat. Add the prawns and fry briskly on both sides until pink and cooked. Add 2 tablespoons of lime juice, tip into a bowl, and set aside.

2 Whisk together 2 tablespoons of lime juice and 6 tablespoons of extra virgin olive oil. Season to taste with the fresh chillies, salt and freshly ground black pepper. Mix half of the dressing into the prawns.

3 Peel each mango with a small knife. Cut its flesh away from the stone in 4 segments and finely slice each segment lengthways. Place in a bowl with the red onion and salad and coriander leaves.

4 Halve, stone and peel the avocados, then slice their flesh lengthways. Dress in the remaining dressing before mixing into the salad with the prawns. Plate, garnished with the lime, and serve immediately.

cherry tomato, basil and roasted pepper salad

Here, a sour vinaigrette is used to enliven a sweet (peppers and mozzarella), umami (tomatoes) and bitter, salty (olives) salad. It tastes gorgeous.

serves 4

2 yellow peppers, quartered and seeded
1 clove of garlic, finely diced
2 tablespoons white wine vinegar
6 tablespoons extra virgin olive oil
salt and freshly ground black pepper
500g (1lb 2oz) baby plum tomatoes, halved
8 fat green olives, stoned and quartered
a handful of fresh basil leaves, ripped
2 buffalo mozzarella cheeses, drained

1 Preheat the grill to its highest setting. Arrange the peppers, skin-side-up, underneath the grill and grill until their skin is blistered and blackened. Transfer to a small bowl and cover until cool enough to handle. Then peel off the skin and cut the peppers into thick strips.

2 Whisk together the garlic, vinegar and olive oil, and season to taste. Place the halved tomatoes in a mixing bowl with the roasted pepper strips, stoned and quartered olives and basil leaves. Mix in the vinaigrette.

3 When ready to serve, cut the mozzarella into thick slices and divide between 4 plates. Season with freshly ground black pepper and arrange the tomato salad to one side of the mozzarella. Serve with lots of crusty white bread to mop up the juices.

lettuce, bacon and quail's egg salad

The classic bitter, sour, salty vinaigrette in this salad will enhance the inherent sweetness of bitter lettuce leaves, green beans, new potatoes, lentils and such like, but it will also bring out any underlying sourness, so do not use on unripe tomatoes or sorrel. This salad's components are carefully chosen to tease the appetite.

serves 4

12 quail's eggs
1 teaspoon Dijon mustard
1 clove of garlic, finely diced
1 tablespoon white wine vinegar
5 tablespoons extra virgin olive oil
salt and freshly ground black pepper
a pinch of caster sugar
4 little gem lettuce hearts, separated and trimmed
4 handfuls of watercress, trimmed
225g (8oz) back bacon, diced

1 Cover the eggs with cold water and bring to the boil. Simmer for 3 minutes, drain and leave in cold water.

2 Whisk together the mustard, garlic, vinegar and 3 tablespoons of extra virgin olive oil in a small bowl. Season, adding a pinch of caster sugar, and set aside.

3 Place the salad leaves in a bowl. Peel and halve the quail's eggs when cool enough to handle and add to the salad leaves. Finally, heat 2 tablespoons of olive oil in a frying pan and briskly fry the diced bacon until crispy. Drain on kitchen paper, add to the salad leaves and gently mix in the mustard vinaigrette. Serve immediately.

marinades

One method of instilling sourness into a dish is to marinate a food in a mildly acidic bath of flavoursome ingredients. Lemon juice, for example, is commonly used as a marinade throughout the Middle East, just as wine is used in much of Europe. The acid tenderizes the flesh of meat and fowl and 'cooks' raw fish by changing its texture. Citrus juice negates any unpleasantly bitter, raw taste and imbues flesh with a freshness that underlines any intrinsic sweetness. If the meat is then subjected to a high heat so that it forms a seal, the sugars in the citrus juice will caramelize, giving the meat an even richer, meatier-tasting crust. Yoghurt is used in much the same way in India, usually combined with lime juice to speed up the tenderization and increase the sourness. Wine, however, can impart a slight bitterness, so care is needed to offset this when stewing or roasting meat. Normally, the inclusion of sweet sautéed vegetables and an umami stock is sufficient.

lemon-marinated lamb kebab

This recipe is an adaptation from Margaret Shaida's wonderful *The Legendary Cuisine of Persia*. The lemon juice negates the bloody bitter taste of the lamb, making it taste fresher and therefore sweeter, while the bitter-sweet saffron butter deepens this sour-sweet taste, thereby creating a scrumptious dish. Note how the bitter-sweet salad adds to this effect.

serves 6

900g (2lb) lean lamb leg steaks
6 lemons, juiced
4 medium onions, roughly grated
salt and freshly ground black pepper
10 threads saffron, ground
115g (4oz) butter, melted

to serve

4 little gem lettuces, separated and ripped
70g (2½oz) watercress, trimmed
a large handful of fresh mint leaves,
finely shredded
18 sandwich-sized pitta bread

1 Cut the lamb into medium-sized cubes. Place the lamb in a colander, wash thoroughly under the cold tap and drain well. In a bowl, mix the lamb with the juice of 4 lemons, the grated onions and the freshly ground black pepper. Cover and chill for 2½ hours.

2 Shortly before serving, grind the saffron stamens under a teaspoon. Dissolve in 1 teaspoon of boiling water and mix in the butter and the juice of 2 lemons. Preheat a barbecue or oven-top grill-pan to medium hot. Mix the salad leaves and herbs in a bowl.

3 Season the meat with salt and thread on to skewers, then lightly coat with some of the lemon butter and grill for 4–6 minutes, or until cooked medium rare. Turn and baste regularly with the lemon butter. Meanwhile, lightly grill the pitta bread, split open and loosely stuff with the salad. As soon as the lamb is cooked, transfer to a bowl, mix in the remaining lemon butter, toss and adjust the seasoning to taste, then stuff into the pitta bread. Serve immediately.

tandoori monkfish

Sour yoghurt-based tandoori marinades can be used for chicken, prawns and various fish. The yoghurt and lime juice bring out the inherent sweetness of the flesh and, in this case, negate any fishy odours. The accompanying sweet-sour Indian mint chutney will amplify this effect even further, thereby creating a very exciting dish. If cooking chicken, stab the meat with a sharp knife before marinating and, if possible, chill for about 6 hours.

serves 4

600g (1lb 5oz) monkfish fillet
4 tablespoons natural Greek yoghurt
1 lime, juiced
1 teaspoon paprika
½ teaspoon ground cumin
1 teaspoon garam masala
1 teaspoon finely chopped fresh ginger
2 small cloves of garlic, crushed
salt and freshly ground black pepper
1 tablespoon sunflower oil

accompaniments

Indian mint chutney (see p.194)
2 red onions, halved and roughly sliced
½ cucumber, peeled and cut into thick slices
½ mooli, peeled and cut into thick slices, or a
bunch of radishes, trimmed and halved
2 limes, cut into wedges

1 Trim the monkfish fillet and cut into large pieces. Mix together the yoghurt, lime juice, spices, ginger and garlic, and season to taste. Add the monkfish. Coat thoroughly, cover and chill. Leave for 40 minutes.

2 Preheat the oven to its highest setting. Line a baking tray with foil and lightly oil. Remove the fish from the marinade and coat it in the remaining oil. Roast for 15 minutes, then serve with the mint chutney and other accompaniments.

sauces

Since sour ingredients combine an intense taste with the ability to enhance any intrinsic sweetness and lessen bitterness or saltiness, they naturally lend themselves to sauces. It is, after all, a quite simple matter for the creative cook to progress from squeezing some lime juice on to food to spooning on a lime sauce. Thus, while the French may question our sanity in eating lamb with a sweet and sour mint sauce, In reality the sauce enhances the meat's inherent sweetness and lessens its muttony odours.

It is, however, worth remembering that any reduction of citrus juice, wine or vinegar will increase both their acidity and sweetness (if present), giving the sauce a vibrant taste when it is diluted with cream, egg yolks or butter.

sorrel sauce with pan-grilled salmon

Sorrel adds a fruity sourness to sauces that works well with the umami sweetness of seared food, regardless of whether it is fish, chicken or veal. Here, sorrel's acidity is diluted and softened by cream.

serves 6

6 x 140g (5oz) salmon fillets
1–2 tablespoons olive oil
salt and freshly ground black pepper
115g (4oz) sorrel
285ml (½ pint) whipping cream
30g (1oz) butter

1 Preheat an oven-top grill-pan over a medium heat. Rub the salmon with some olive oil and season to taste. Place flesh-side-down on the grill-pan and cook for 4 minutes. Then lift gently and reposition, still flesh-side-down, so that the flesh is seared with golden, diamond, criss-cross grill lines. After 4 minutes, turn skin-side-down and cook for 4 minutes, until just rosy inside.

2 Meanwhile, fold together the 2 edges of each sorrel leaf and rip away the stalk, then finely slice the leaves. Bring the cream up to the boil in a small saucepan. At the same time melt the butter in a small pan and stir in the shredded sorrel. As soon as it has collapsed into soggy, khaki-coloured shreds, stir the sorrel into the cream. Simmer gently for 10 minutes, season to taste, then serve with the fish.

citrus butter sauce with grilled sea bass

Reducing a sour ingredient in a sauce is also a useful way to infuse flavour — as in the recipe below. Thus, lime juice can be infused and reduced with ginger or white wine with shallot and tarragon. This sauce has an intense fruity, sour taste which enhances the delicate sweetness of the fish.

serves 4

juice of ½ lime
juice of 1 lemon
juice of 1½ oranges
1 shallot, finely diced
2 tablespoons double cream
salt and freshly ground black pepper
2 x 800g (1¾lb) sea bass, filleted
3 tablespoons olive oil
200g (7oz) chilled unsalted butter, diced

1 Place the lime, lemon and orange juice in a small non-corrosive saucepan with the finely diced shallot. Boil vigorously until it has reduced to about 3 tablespoons of intense-tasting liquid. Add the double cream, season to taste and set aside.

2 Preheat an oven-top grill-pan (or barbecue) to medium high. Trim the sea bass fillets, brush with olive oil, and place flesh-side-down on the grill-pan or barbecue. Cook for 3 minutes, then carefully turn them over and grill the skin side for 4 minutes.

3 Bring the citrus juice sauce to the boil, then reduce the heat to a low simmer and gradually whisk in the butter, one piece at a time, so that it emulsifies as it melts. Do not let it boil, or it may split. Remove and serve with the fish.

savoury dishes

When considering how the five tastes affect one another, it is a small step to progress from separate sauces to integrated dishes. The main difference is that the impact of a particular taste has to be slightly softened in an integrated dish, as usually the taste is cooked and absorbed into the other ingredients rather than being served as a separate, contrasting dish. The basic principles, however, remain the same – namely that umami and sweetness will negate sourness, while a hint of saltiness or bitterness will highlight it, along with any sweetness.

Most 'sour' savoury dishes fall into one of two categories: sweet and sour or sour and bitter. Both contain salt, as it intensifies sourness and sweetness while counterbalancing bitterness. In effect, these two combinations are very satisfying to eat and will bring out any innate sweetness and saltiness in the main ingredient, as can be seen with the sea bass in tamarind (see p.36) or the lemon and olive chicken tagine (see p.39).

pappardelle with mushrooms, wine and herbs

This dish spans the line between an integrated dish and a separate sauce. The mushrooms can be served as a sauce to grilled chicken, veal or white fish. The sauce is given greater intensity by the reduction of the wine, which cuts down the sweetness of the sautéed shallots and brings out the bitter-sweet nature of the mushrooms. The herbs add further aromatic notes which, like all 'flavours', are picked up by olfactory, rather than taste, cells.

serves 2

3 tablespoons olive oil
2 small shallots, finely diced
1 small clove of garlic, finely chopped
85g (3oz) shiitake mushrooms, de-stalked and ripped
115g (4oz) brown cap mushrooms, trimmed and thickly sliced
85g (3oz) oyster mushrooms, trimmed and ripped
100ml (3.5fl oz) dry white wine
a handful of finely chopped fresh parsley, chives and thyme leaves
salt and freshly ground black pepper
30g (1oz) unsalted butter
140g (5oz) dried pappardelle or tagliatelle

1 Pour the olive oil in a frying pan, add the shallots and garlic and gently sauté until they are soft and golden. Mix in the shiitake and brown cap mushrooms. After a minute add the oyster mushrooms. Once they begin to soften, stir in the white wine, herbs and seasoning. Allow the mixture to bubble up and reduce by half. Swirl the butter into the mushrooms, so that it thickens their juices a little.

2 Meanwhile, drop the pasta into boiling salted water. Cook until it is *al dente* – the time will vary according to the make of pasta. Drain, mix in the mushroom sauce and serve immediately.

sweet and sour chicken

It would have been impossible to write a book on taste and not include an interpretation of a Chinese sweet and sour sauce. Here, the acidity is found in the vinegar; the salt and umami in the soy sauce; and the sweetness in the sugar. The tomato ketchup contains all five tastes. This combination of ingredients adds up to a very gratifying dish.

serves 4

450g (1lb) boned and skinned chicken breasts
1 tablespoon rice wine
4 tablespoons soy sauce
2 teaspoons sesame oil
3 tablespoons cornflour, plus extra for dusting
1 medium egg, beaten
salt
sunflower oil for deep-frying, plus 2 tablespoons
4 tablespoons soft light brown sugar
2 tablespoons tomato ketchup
6 tablespoons rice or white wine vinegar
1 red pepper, quartered, seeded and cut into large dice
1 small red onion, cut into large dice
1 small clove of garlic, finely diced
225g can of pineapple chunks, drained

1 Cut the chicken into 2.5cm (1-inch) cubes. Marinate in the rice wine, 1 tablespoon soy sauce and the sesame oil for 20 minutes. Meanwhile, measure 2 tablespoons of cornflour into another bowl and beat in the egg with a fork to make a smooth batter. Season with salt and set aside.

2 Preheat the oil in a deep fat fryer to 190°C (375°F). Meanwhile, make the sauce by mixing together 1 heaped tablespoon of cornflour with 4 tablespoons of cold water. Then mix this with the brown sugar, ketchup, vinegar and 3 tablespoons of soy sauce.

3 Drain the chicken, dust in cornflour, dip in batter and carefully drop half into the hot oil. Deep fry for 2 minutes, or until golden. Remove and drain on kitchen paper. Repeat the process with the remaining diced chicken.

4 Preheat a wok or non-stick frying pan. Add 2 tablespoons of sunflower oil and when it is very hot, add the red pepper, red onion and garlic. Stir fry for 30 seconds, then add the chicken and pineapple chunks, quickly followed by the sauce. Boil vigorously until it has thickened slightly. Serve immediately with steamed rice.

almond beef curry with yoghurt

Any dish that contains slowly fried or roasted onions, shallots or garlic can taste very sweet, as their sugars caramelize as they cook. The solution is to add some form of acidity to counteract the sweetness. The result can be amazingly moreish, as with this curry, where the taste buds are stimulated by that irresistible combination of sweet, sour and salt plus spice.

serves 6

2 dried Kashmiri chillies
1 teaspoon cumin seeds
1 teaspoon black peppercorns
½ small cinnamon stick, broken
10 cardamom pods
1 kg (2lb 3oz) trimmed and diced Aberdeen Angus braising steak
7 tablespoons sunflower oil
400g (14oz) onions, finely sliced
3 cloves of garlic, finely chopped
1 teaspoon finely chopped fresh ginger
285ml (½ pint) natural Greek yoghurt
1 bay leaf
2 teaspoons sea salt
225g (8oz) plain flour
55g (2oz) ground almonds
a pinch of dried chilli flakes for garnish

1 Set a small frying pan over a low heat and gently dry roast the chillies until they are slightly coloured. Set aside. Add the cumin seeds, black peppercorns, cinnamon and cardamom pods and roast until they release a wonderful scent. Tip them into a spice grinder with the chillies and grind until they form a fine powder. Mix into the trimmed and diced meat with a tablespoon of sunflower oil. Cover and chill for 3–6 hours.

2 Preheat the oven to 150°C (300°F) gas mark 2. Heat 3 tablespoons of oil in a flameproof casserole dish or ovenproof saucepan. Add the onions and gently fry over a medium-low heat for 10 minutes, or until soft and golden. Then mix in the garlic and ginger and fry for 5 minutes before adding 3 tablespoons of oil and the meat. Increase the heat and stir briskly until the meat is thoroughly browned. Whisk the yoghurt with about 225ml (8fl oz) water and stir into the beef with the bay leaf and salt. Bring up to a simmer and remove from the heat.

3 Make a flour paste by mixing the flour with 140ml (¼ pint) cold water to form a firm dough. Roll it into a long sausage and press it around the rim of the saucepan or casserole dish. Squash on the lid so it is tightly sealed. Place in the oven and bake for 1½ hours.

4 Crack open the crisp paste and prise off the lid. Mix in the almonds and transfer the curry to a clean pan. Reheat thoroughly and serve garnished with the dried chilli flakes when you're ready.

spiced tamarind chickpeas

The fruity sour nature of tamarind makes it work well with other sweet-sour fruits such as tomatoes.

serves 4

225g (8oz) dried chickpeas
¾ teaspoon bicarbonate of soda
20g (¾oz) tamarind pulp (with seeds)
1 medium onion, sliced
3 tablespoons sunflower oil
2 cloves of garlic, finely chopped
2 teaspoons finely chopped fresh ginger
1 green chilli, finely sliced
1 teaspoon turmeric
1 teaspoon garam masala
130g (4½oz) ripe tomatoes, peeled and chopped
a handful of fresh coriander, stems and leaves separated and stems finely chopped

1 Soak the chickpeas in cold water overnight. Drain and place in a saucepan. Cover with cold water, bring up to the boil, skimming regularly, and boil vigorously for 10 minutes. Add the bicarbonate of soda and cook at a gentle boil for 40 minutes, or until the chickpeas are meltingly soft. Leave in their cooking liquid. Soak the tamarind pulp in 140ml (¼ pint) of the hot chickpea cooking liquid. After 15 minutes, loosen the tamarind pulp from the stones and strain through a coarse sieve.

2 Fry the onion briskly in the oil, stirring regularly, for 4 minutes, until it has caramelized. Lower the heat and stir in the garlic, ginger and chilli. After 3 minutes, mix in the spices and fry for 2 minutes. Stir in the tomatoes and coriander stalks and cook vigorously until dark and thick and the oil separates from the sauce. Drain the chickpeas, saving their liquid, and mix into the tomatoes with the strained tamarind juice. Cover with their cooking water and simmer for 30 minutes. Serve with a scattering of fresh, roughly sliced coriander leaves.

sea bass in tamarind

This is a delicious example of one of the many sweet, sour and salt variations in cooking.

serves 4

2 tablespoons tamarind pulp (with seeds)
2 tablespoons light brown muscovado sugar
3 tablespoons soy sauce
1½ tablespoons fish sauce (nam pla)
4 x 450g (1lb) sea bass, filleted and skinned
3 tablespoons sunflower oil
2 tablespoons finely shredded fresh ginger
3 cloves of garlic, finely chopped
6 spring onions, finely sliced
a large handful of fresh coriander leaves

1 Place the tamarind and 9 tablespoons of warm water in a bowl. Loosen the pulp around the stones and soak for 15 minutes. Strain, pushing through any pulp, and mix with the sugar, soy sauce and fish sauce. Set aside.

2 Fry half the fish fillets, flesh-side-down, in the oil for 1–2 minutes. Turn over and repeat. Remove. Repeat with the remaining fish. Stir-fry the ginger for a few seconds, add the garlic, stir-fry for a few seconds more, then add the tamarind sauce. Boil for a minute, then return the fish to the pan with the spring onions. Heat, sprinkle with coriander, and serve with steamed rice.

lamb daube

Wine-based stews are all examples of sour, bitter and salt combinations. The wine has an element of bitterness, which the meat can absorb in its marinade. Here, this is subtly increased by the addition of dried orange peel and brandy. Sealing the meat in olive oil, which is intrinsically bitter, rather than in neutral sunflower oil, would add even more bitterness, while browning and the stock introduces a hint of umami, which will enhance the sweetness of the sautéed vegetables, thereby softening the acidity. The bacon adds salt.

serves 6

1kg (2lb 3oz) trimmed and diced leg of lamb

marinade

1 bottle of good red wine, such as a Pinot Noir
1 bay leaf
3 sprigs of fresh thyme
1 large sprig of fresh parsley
1 onion, roughly sliced
1 clove of garlic, roughly sliced
2 outer sticks of celery, roughly sliced
2 large carrots, peeled and sliced
3 cloves
5 black peppercorns

daube

3 strips of finely pared orange peel
5 tablespoons sunflower oil
225g (8oz) smoked back bacon, cut into lardons
2 onions, quartered and sliced
3 carrots, peeled and cut into batons
1 small clove of garlic, finely chopped
2 tablespoons good brandy
225g (8oz) plain flour, plus 1 tablespoon
140ml (¼ pint) good lamb or chicken stock
3 stems of fresh parsley
2 sprigs of fresh thyme
salt and freshly ground black pepper
2 tablespoons finely chopped fresh parsley

1 Mix the diced lamb in a china bowl with all the marinade ingredients. Cover and chill for 12 hours.

2 Heat the oven to 140°C (275°F) gas mark 1. Put the orange peel into the oven and remove when curled and dry. Meanwhile, drain the marinated meat, saving its juices. Separate the meat from the marinated vegetables, herbs and spices, and set both aside.

3 Heat 2 tablespoons of oil in a frying pan over a moderate heat. Sauté the bacon for 3 minutes, then add the onions, carrots and garlic. Once the onions are soft and golden, transfer to a casserole dish.

4 Add 2 tablespoons of oil to the frying pan and increase the heat to high. Briskly fry a single layer of marinated lamb until well coloured, then transfer to the casserole dish. Repeat the process with the remaining meat. Warm the brandy, then pour it over the lamb in the casserole dish, set alight and mix well.

5 Tip the drained marinated vegetables into the frying pan and sauté until soft. Stir in a tablespoon of flour, cook for 2 minutes, then mix in the reserved marinade and boil vigorously until it has reduced by half. Strain into the casserole, add the stock, dried orange peel, parsley stems and thyme and season to taste.

6 Make a paste with the plain flour and about 140ml (¼ pint) of water. Roll it into a long sausage, press around the rim of the casserole and squash on the lid. Bake for 1 hour 20 minutes. Then break the seal, add the chopped parsley and serve. This is lovely with a 'sweet' celeriac and potato purée.

lemon and olive chicken tagine

In this sour, bitter and salt recipe, the olives and preserved lemons (see p.77) both add bitterness and saltiness which imbue the dish with an intriguing sweet-sour intensity. The same concept can be applied to other meats, such as lamb, partridge or guinea fowl.

It is important to soak the olives before cooking to reduce their bitterness. In Morocco, a generous tablespoon of *smen* (preserved semi-rancid butter) is used in place of ordinary butter. This adds another layer of acidity.

serves 6

300g (10½oz) green Moroccan or Greek olives, pitted and drained weight
1 large free-range oven-ready chicken
2 tablespoons fine sea salt
3 small preserved lemons, rinsed, halved and seeded
5 tablespoons vegetable oil
15g (½oz) butter
4 large red onions, roughly sliced
4 cloves of garlic, roughly chopped
a pinch of freshly ground black pepper
1½ teaspoons ground cumin
2 teaspoons ground ginger
a small bunch of fresh flat-leaf parsley, roughly chopped
a small bunch of fresh coriander, roughly chopped
3 tablespoons lemon juice

1 Wash the olives and leave to soak in cold water while you prepare the chicken. Cut the chicken into 10 pieces (including the chicken wings). Each breast should be attached to its bone and divided into two. Rinse under the cold tap, then rub each piece with sea salt – partially lift up the skin and pull away any fat or membrane that might lie underneath as you do so. Then rinse lightly before rubbing each piece with two of the halved lemons. Set aside for 10 minutes.

2 Meanwhile, drain the olives. Tip into a saucepan, cover with plenty of cold water and simmer gently for 15 minute, then drain.

3 Place the oil, butter, onion, garlic, spices, chicken pieces, parsley and all but 2 tablespoons of coriander in a large saucepan. Set over a medium high heat and mix thoroughly. Stir regularly until the chicken is lightly coloured – this will take about 10 minutes – then add 285ml (½ pint) cold water. Cover, reduce the temperature to a simmer and cook gently for 30 minutes, turning the chicken regularly.

4 Mix in the drained olives and remaining preserved lemon. Simmer for 20 minutes, or until the chicken is tender. Skim off the excess fat, add the lemon juice and reserved fresh coriander and season to taste. Transfer to a dish, spooning the olives and juices all around the meat. Rip the preserved lemon into several pieces and place on top.

puddings

Just as sourness stimulates the appetite, so sweetness ultimately satisfies it. They perfectly complement one another. In other words, if you want to make a pleasing pudding, you cannot go far wrong by sweetening a sour ingredient. However, their contradictory nature has a further effect, which is to refresh the eater, as can be discovered by eating a lemon or raspberry sorbet. If you add salt or bitterness, it seems to complicate the different tastes and dull their exquisite, clean taste. A hint of bitterness, however, can work very well if a dish like rhubarb fool is sweetened by more complex-tasting ingredients, such as cream. Curiously, only sweet bitterness really satisfies the appetite, which is probably why people drink sweetened espresso coffee and nibble chocolates or bitter almond ratafias at the end of a meal.

Sour ingredients are often used in puddings to enhance another ingredient. Wine, for example, is frequently reduced, sweetened and infused with other flavourings to bring out the sweet-sour nature of fruit. Similarly, other acids might be used to enhance more subtle-tasting fruits, such as strawberries drizzled with a sweet-sour balsamic vinegar, or blackberries baked in a gooey lemon pudding. Needless to say, their intrinsic sourness becomes vibrant when sweetened.

peaches in white wine

This sour-sweet syrup can be used with quinces, pears or nectarines. Remember that both its acidity and its sweetness will increase with reduction.

serves 6

565ml (1 pint) white wine
½ vanilla pod, split
5 black peppercorns
170g (6oz) granulated sugar
4 finely pared strips of lemon peel, plus juice of ½ lemon
6 medium peaches

1 Place the wine, 140ml (¼ pint) water, vanilla pod, black peppercorns, sugar and lemon peel in a non-corrosive saucepan. Dissolve the sugar over a moderate heat.

2 Halve and stone the peaches. Drop half of them, cut-side-up, into the hot syrup and cover with a crumpled sheet of greaseproof paper, so that the peaches are not exposed to the air. Simmer briskly for 12 minutes, or until tender. Remove with a slotted spoon and place in a shallow dish, skin-side-up. Peel, return their skins to the simmering syrup along with the remaining peaches, and repeat the process.

3 Once all the peaches are peeled, add the lemon juice to the syrup and boil vigorously for 15 minutes, or until reduced by more than two-thirds. Strain over the peaches and leave to cool. Serve at room temperature, or chilled, with crème fraîche or clotted cream.

apple and sorrel fritters

Sorrel was once used in place of lemon juice in English cooking. Its fresh, sappy sourness, when mixed with a little sugar, enhances both the sweetness and sourness of apples, making them taste amazingly fruity. Compare this with a plain apple fritter.

serves 4

85g (3oz) fresh sorrel
45g (1½oz) caster sugar
3 medium eating apples
sunflower oil
115g (4oz) plain flour
a pinch of salt
2 egg whites
extra caster sugar to serve

1 Wash and dry the sorrel. Rip away the stems by folding together the 2 edges of each leaf and pulling away the stem from the leaf. Finely chop the leaves and mix with the sugar in a bowl. Peel, quarter and core the apples, then halve each quarter. Coat in the sorrel sugar and leave to macerate.

2 Preheat the oil in a deep fat fryer to 190°C (375°F). Sift the flour and salt into a bowl and slowly stir in 140ml (¼ pint) water so it forms a thick, smooth batter. Whisk the egg whites until they form stiff peaks. Using a metal spoon, lightly fold them into the batter.

3 Making sure each apple segment is covered in sorrel, dip into the batter, then drop into the oil and cook in batches. Fry for 3 minutes, flipping them over half-way, until the batter is puffy and the palest gold. Drain on kitchen paper, then arrange on a warm plate. Liberally sprinkle with caster sugar and serve at once.

rhubarb almond fool

Bitterness can add a sophisticated intensity to creamy sweet-sour puddings.

serves 6

450g (1lb) rhubarb (prepared weight)
granulated sugar to taste
285ml (½ pint) double cream
a few drops of natural almond essence

1 Trim the rhubarb, discarding the tops and bottoms. Wash and cut into medium chunks. Place in a non-corrosive saucepan with 4 tablespoons of sugar and 2 tablespoons water. Cook gently over a low heat until the rhubarb is tender but not completely disintegrated. Add about 85g (3oz) sugar to taste and leave until cold.

2 Whisk the cream into soft peaks, then gradually fold in the rhubarb with its juice. Season to taste with natural almond essence. Spoon into delicate glasses and serve with bitter-sweet macaroons.

preserves

Sourness is a major factor in many preserves. Aside from the practicalities of eliminating bacteria by preserving food in vinegar, or ensuring that a jam sets by hastening the release of pectin in fruit so that it can react with sugar to form a gel, acidity also counteracts the intense taste of sugar or salt necessary for preservation.

Preserves can be sweet and sour as below; sweet, sour and bitter, as with pickled red cabbage or damson jelly; or even sour, salty and bitter, as with sauerkraut or green mango pickle. Their vivid taste is best utilized as an accompaniment to other foods; like a sauce, the taste of a preserve will enhance other ingredients. The skill of the cook partly lies in offering the most appropriate taste combination – sweet pickled quinces, for instance, work particularly well with a lemony young goat's cheese or a slightly bitter, wine-marinated roast venison.

sweet pickled quince

Quince have an exquisite aroma that is an exotic mix of flowers and spices. Amazingly, this can be partially captured by cooking them – even in a strong-tasting, sweet-sour pickle. Here, the flavours of the spices and lemon zest are used to enhance this aroma.

makes 2 x 500g (1lb 2oz) Kilner jars

600ml (21fl oz) perry (pear) or cider vinegar
800g (1¾lb) granulated sugar
6 allspice berries
3 cloves
6 black peppercorns
3 dried Kashmiri (or other mild) chillies
1 lemon, finely pared and juiced
1.8kg (4lb) quince

1 Place the vinegar, sugar, spices and finely pared lemon peel in a non-corrosive saucepan. Dissolve the sugar over a low heat and simmer gently. Meanwhile, peel, quarter and core the quince, cut into segments and mix in the lemon juice as you go along. Transfer the fruit (without the lemon juice) to the spiced syrup and simmer for about 30 minutes, or until tender. The time will vary according to the ripeness of the quince.

2 Preheat the oven to 140°C (275°F) gas mark 1. Sterilize the Kilner jars by washing in warm soapy water, rinsing and placing in the preheated oven for 10 minutes or until dry. Boil any lids or rubber seals for a minute or two, then allow to dry.

3 Using a slotted spoon, slip the quince segments into the hot jars. Boil the remaining syrup until it has reduced by a third. Remove the chillies (unless you like very hot pickles) and pour over the syrup to cover the fruit. Seal while hot. Label and store in a cool, dark place. They will be ready after a month, if you can resist them for that long, but improve with age.

sour notes

Tart fruit curds such as passion fruit, lemon, orange or raspberry can be spread on to cakes, roulades or tarts to add a tempting sour bite to their sweetness.

A last-minute spoonful of soured cream, buttermilk or crème fraîche will add a refreshing sour note to soups by reducing their natural sweetness. Try swirling soured cream into puréed beetroot soup, crème fraîche into spiced parsnip or sweet potato soup, or buttermilk into spinach or apple and butternut soup.

Savoury tarts can be transformed into irresistible morsels by substituting soured cream or crème fraîche in place of ordinary cream when making their egg custard. The delicate sourness of the cream cuts down the sweetness of the sautéed onions or leeks and enhances the other ingredients such as bacon, mushrooms or spinach.

A squeeze of lime or lemon juice will make sweet fruit such as papaya or melon taste even more luscious, especially if it is lightly seasoned with a hint of black pepper and salt. It is also worth trying citrus fruit on sweet vegetables – grilled sweetcorn, in particular, tastes fantastic rubbed with lime or lemon and a touch of salt, black pepper and amchoor (an Indian fruity-sour dried mango powder).

Sweet, buttery cakes or rum babas will release all their subtle flavours if drenched in a sour sugar-syrup. The zingy fresh acidity of lime, lemon or Seville orange juice lessens the natural sweetness of the sponge while emphasizing other flavours such as almonds or vanilla. Simply mix the fresh juice into a sugar-syrup – infused with bitter peel if you wish – and use as needed. A dash of alcohol, such as rum, gin or vodka, will give an added kick to the sourness of the sugar-syrup.

Yoghurt drizzled over lamb or chicken kebabs in salad-stuffed pitta breads will make them taste all the more alluring. Use good-quality natural Greek yoghurt, thin to taste with a little water and season with salt. If a hint of bitterness is required, toast some cumin seeds in a dry frying pan, grind and sprinkle over the sauce.

A dab of lemon butter melted on to some grilled or fried fish, chicken or meat will instantly imbue it with an alluring sour taste. Simply beat together 55g (2oz) softened, unsalted butter with 2 teaspoons of lemon juice, a pinch of cayenne pepper, salt and freshly ground black pepper. Adjust to taste and roll into a smooth sausage in wet greaseproof paper. Chill and cut as needed. If you are feeling suave, add a hint of bitterness with 3 finely chopped green olives, or a little fragrance with some finely chopped tarragon or thyme.

Salsas are another good way to introduce a tantalizing sweet sourness to an unsour dish. Tomato, garlic and basil salsa (made with a vinaigrette), or mango and papaya salsa seasoned with lime juice, coriander and chilli, for example, will enliven fish, chicken or meat.

Sour dipping sauces are a useful way to add a sour note to 'dry' dishes such as deep-fried spring rolls or grilled prawns. One of my favourites is this sweet-sour chilli vinegar sauce. Pour 5 tablespoons of boiling water on to 2 tablespoons of granulated sugar and ½ teaspoon of dried chilli flakes. Stir until the sugar has dissolved. Add 2½ tablespoons of white wine vinegar, ½ cucumber, peeled, seeded and finely diced, and season to taste with salt. For an aromatic sauce, omit the cucumber and add a finely sliced stem of lemon grass with the chilli. Its sweet-sourness will enliven and amplify any sweet tastes in the dish.

salt

Salt is as essential to life as water. Its taste permeates all our meals, despite the fact that there are few naturally salty foods. Until recently, it was thought that we only had four tastes, but now research indicates that we have a fifth – the Japanese call it umami, derived from the Japanese *umai*, meaning delicious. This taste is always present in foods that contain high levels of free glutamate (a common amino acid). Umami is typified by the intense, savoury and pleasurable taste you get from soy sauce, reduced chicken broth or a mature cheese such as Parmesan. It is often found in salty or cured foods such as Stilton or Parma ham. Thus, both tastes are covered in this chapter.

Ironically, the less salt we eat, the more salt we can taste in food. I used to be sceptical about such matters, until I reduced my own salt intake. After a few uncomfortable weeks, I began to detect amazing nuances of taste in everything I ate. Even tomatoes seemed salty. In fact, over-salting dulls our perception of all five tastes, so it is important to learn how to manipulate it for maximum effect.

Most salty foods are man-made and were developed to preserve various ingredients, such as meat, fish and cheese. They needed careful handling to reduce their saltiness, usually by soaking, blanching or dilution. Salty foods are always added to unsalted recipes in small quantities. Sweetness appears to lessen saltiness, while bitterness and umami increase it. A little sourness emphasizes saltiness but, where an ingredient is salty-sweet, sourness enhances the sweetness and, in doing so, counteracts the saltiness, as can be learnt by eating a salted anchovy fillet with a few drops of lemon.

Relatively little is known about how umami affects the other tastes. It is thought that it accentuates the savoury nature of other foods; imagine the taste of steamed rice with and without soy sauce. Umami seems to heighten our sensitivity towards saltiness and sweetness, and lessen our awareness of sour and bitter tastes. It certainly increases salivation, a fact not lost on food manufacturers who widely use monosodium glutamate (MSG), a manufactured chemical flavour enhancer, to artificially add umami to their products. Everything from stock cubes to oyster sauce can contain it! A significant number of people have physical reactions to MSG, but curiously the problem appears to be less pronounced in foods that naturally contain free glutamate. This may be because it is then consumed in very small quantities, thus allowing cooks to benefit from its savoury nature.

Cooking, like any other art, depends upon the sensitivity of the cook, and in no instance is this more true than with the use of salt and umami (I am not referring to MSG here, which is an additive I would happily ban). The lightest hand will create the most subtle and scrumptious dishes where the eater detects not the salt nor the umami, but the delicate natural taste of the food itself.

soy sauce

Cooks have long appreciated the salty umami taste of soy sauce. The best soy sauce is brewed naturally by a complex process of slowly fermenting de-fatted soy beans with roasted wheat and several cultures of *Aspergillus* moulds, before adding a strong salt solution and further cultures. Soy sauce contains glutamic acid and volatile aromatic substances. The result, according to Hsiang Ju Lin and Tsuifeng Lin in *Chinese Gastronomy* (1969), imparts a meaty taste and colour to meat, soups and sauces.

Soy sauce varies depending on how and where it's brewed. A good Chinese soy sauce, for example, is more intense and salty than an equally well made, slightly sweeter, Japanese version. All have an affinity with sweet foods such as fish or honey, and work well balanced with acidic tastes such as saké. Soy sauce also enhances sweetness in bitter foods.

parmesan

As Elizabeth David wrote in *Spices, Salt and Aromatics in the English Kitchen* (1975), Parmesan cheese is "possessed of the remarkable seasoning powers, seasoning without overpowering". No doubt this is because 100g of Parmesan contains 1200mg of natural free glutamate, compared to the 2mg found in 100g of cow's milk.

Parmesan's correct name is Parmigiano-Reggiano. It is made from unpasteurized, semi-skimmed cow's milk that has been matured for at least 18 months after pressing and salting in a brine bath. Parmesan should have a crumbly texture, a straw colour and a slightly salty, mellow taste. Its salty, umami nature adds excitement to bland sweet foods such as pasta, and depth to sour dishes such as Bolognaise sauce. Parmesan reduces bitterness by emphasizing any sweetness in bitter foods such as basil in pesto sauce.

sea salt

To appreciate the taste of sea salt, allow a couple of coarse crystals to dissolve on your tongue. Salt – sodium chloride, (NaCl) – is commonly seen as a means of adding taste or texture to food. Salt's powers of preservation have given it almost mythical importance in previous ages, but today it is widely regarded as an easy taste enhancer that hits the headlines when chefs ban it from their customers' tables. In reality perception of taste and aroma can differ widely from one person to another, just as perception of colour can vary.

Salt is obtained by mining (rock salt) or by evaporating sea water (sea salt). The latter salt goes under many names, including bay salt, Maldon sea salt, *sel de gris* and *fleur de sel*. These indicate where and how the salt has been evaporated. Sea salts taste marginally different if they contain trace elements of other minerals.

seaweed

Undulating ribbons of kelp (*Laminaria longicruris*) and rippling fronds of wakame (*Undaria pinnatifida*) and nori (*Porphyra tenera*) conjure up the taste of the sea. Rich in iodine and glutamic acid, seaweed adds a complex umami taste to recipes. The Japanese utilize this in a savoury stock called *dashi*, which is made by infusing water with kelp (*kombu*) and dried bonito flakes (also rich in free glutamate).

All three seaweeds are commonly bought dried. Sheets of nori benefit from being lightly toasted, while wakame needs to be soaked for 20 minutes and trimmed of its tough ribs before being used in soups and salads. Seaweed's saline taste enhances sweet ingredients such as prawns and tofu, and bitter-sweet foods such as shiitake mushrooms or aubergine. Seaweed tastes sweeter if combined with other salty foods such as soy sauce.

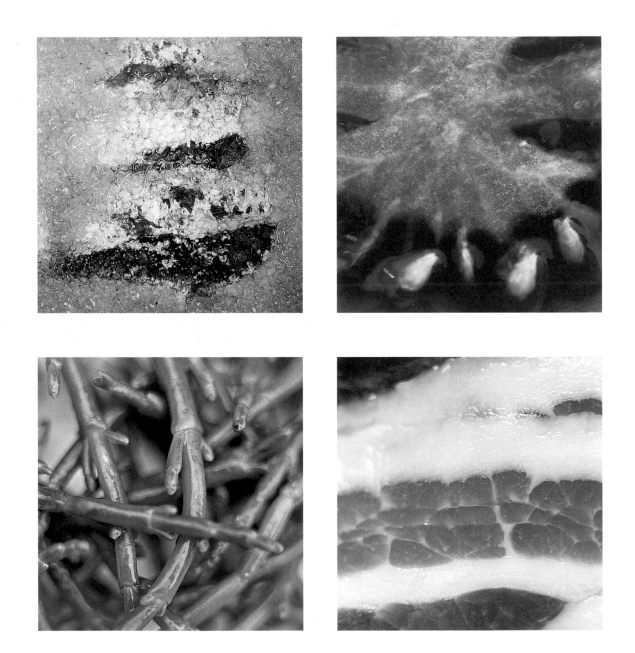

salted anchovies

Plump, rose-fleshed salted anchovies taste intensely salty in a piscine sort of a way. Yet, lard a piece of lamb or beef with a few strips of anchovy fillet and their fishy nature transforms itself into a savoury saltiness that enhances the taste of the meat. Chop them into a simple warm olive oil sauce, and they will infuse it with a lingering salty fishiness that draws out the sweetness of pasta or borlotti beans.

Salted anchovies are normally sold either whole and packed in sea salt, or filleted in olive oil. The former are the best, but are sold in very large tins. In either case, you can diminish their saltiness by rinsing the fillets and soaking them in milk for 20 minutes. The salty nature of anchovies will enhance the sweetness of naturally bitter-sweet foods such as cauliflower, courgette, fennel, lemon zest and mayonnaise, by counteracting their bitterness.

marsh samphire

The plump, segmented green stems of marsh samphire (*Salicornia europaea*) are filled with a delicate saline juice that tempt the eater to take one salty yet refreshing bite after another. It grows wild on the mineral-rich mud flats and salt marshes near the sea, but is sometimes confused in cookery books with rock samphire (*Crithmum maritimum*), a different plant entirely. Marsh samphire is also known as glasswort in Britain and chicken claws in North America. Fishmongers and health food shops sell the home-grown crop in Britain from June onwards.

Samphire subtly adds a salty, textural element to dishes. It can be eaten raw or cooked. Its salinity perfectly enhances the natural sweetness of lamb, beef and fish, but avoid using with white meat like chicken or pork, as its maritime qualities can emphasise any fishy notes in their flesh.

tomatoes

The tomato is a remarkably savoury fruit and contains an extraordinary combination of tastes. Aside from the fact that it is sweet, sour, salty and bitter, it is also umami, as it contains 200mg of free glutamate per 100g of tomato. This taste combination no doubt accounts for its being one of the most important fruits in the world. Although a vinaigrette is often used to amplify the taste of tomatoes, the bitterness of a superb olive oil and the prickly flavour of black pepper can work equally well. To ensure maximum taste and aroma, store tomatoes at room temperature.

Cooked or raw, tomatoes will enhance the taste of most savoury foods, bringing out their sweet, sour and salt tastes respectively, while counterbalancing any bitterness. Some chefs maintain that tomatoes are also good in puddings, although I have yet to taste an appetizing example.

bacon

Bacon is one of the most versatile of salted foods. It imbues a dish with a delectable hint of salty meatiness. It is made from the entire side of a pig, except its legs. The different cuts – streaky, middle back and back bacon – come from the different parts of the side and contain varying degrees of fat. Back bacon is the leanest, while streaky, which comes from the rib end, contains the most fat and tastes the sweetest. Animal fat is sweeter than lean meat.

Bacon gains its salty taste from being cured in either dry salt (dry cure) or brine (wet cure). It can be sweetened with sugar or treacle, flavoured with spices or smoked. Bacon's salty nature enhances sweetness, for example, in eggs or peas, just as it intensifies our perception of sourness in a wine sauce. Bacon also counteracts bitterness, for example when cooked with game, cabbage or lettuce.

soups

The art of cooking lies in understanding the tastes and how to combine them to enhance a dish. It is, however, equally important to fit the dish to the mood of the occasion. This, again, can be achieved by taste, as different combinations fulfil different needs. Soup, for example, is usually eaten to stimulate the appetite and refresh the palate, although when consumed as a main course it should also satisfy. Consequently, salt and umami are critical tastes when making soup, as the latter, in particular, ensures that it is both stimulating and satisfying.

In reality, most cooks already use both tastes. The intense sweet-salty taste of a good home-made stock is actually that of umami. So is the taste of the Japanese stock dashi, which is made from kelp and dried bonito flakes. Umami adds an appetizing note to the dish and enhances the savoury-sweet taste of the other ingredients. Thus the vegetables and pasta in a minestrone made with chicken stock will taste sweeter and more delectable. Add Parmesan and the umami effect will be increased further. However, since umami can reduce sourness or bitterness, it is sometimes necessary to reinforce that aspect of a recipe to make it taste more stimulating and interesting. Crème fraîche, for example, is added to the sorrel and lettuce soup on p.23 to re-emphasize the sorrel's acidity.

Salt has a gentler effect. If used in moderation, it will amplify the other tastes by enhancing any intrinsic sweetness, sourness and bitterness in a recipe. Beware, however, of using it excessively, as too much salt has the opposite effect of dulling all the tastes before ultimately making a dish unpalatable.

butternut squash and parmesan soup

A clever way to stimulate the taste buds and add a salty-umami depth to a recipe is to add Parmesan. Here, Parmesan rind is simmered with chicken stock and naturally sweet sautéed onions and butternut squash. The stock and Parmesan give the soup a delicate savoury-sweet taste, while the sweetness of the vegetables is reduced a little by crème fraîche. The chilli adds a sensory kick. The result is a sweet-savoury soup that makes a satisfying light main course, since it contains no bitterness and little sourness.

serves 6

2 onions, roughly chopped
1 clove of garlic, roughly chopped
½ teaspoon chilli flakes or to taste (optional)
3 tablespoons olive oil
2 medium butternut squash
1 litre (1¾ pints) chicken stock
1 bay leaf
3 sprigs of fresh parsley
70g (2½oz) piece of Parmesan cheese rind
115ml (4fl oz) crème fraîche
salt and freshly ground black pepper
roughly shaved Parmesan cheese to serve

1 Gently fry the onions, garlic and chilli flakes in the olive oil in a large saucepan for about 10 minutes, or until soft and golden. Meanwhile, cut off the tough skin of the butternut squash. Scrape out and discard the seeds, then roughly dice the flesh and stir it into the sautéed onions. Cover and continue to cook, stirring occasionally, until the squash begins to soften.

2 Add the stock, herbs and Parmesan rind and simmer gently for 45 minutes, or until the squash is meltingly soft. Discard the herbs and Parmesan rind, scraping any gooey cheese into the soup. Liquidize the soup, add the crème fraîche, and season to taste. Serve piping hot scattered with Parmesan cheese shavings.

minestrone

This recipe uses pancetta, Parmesan rind and tomatoes instead of stock. Their salty-umami taste fuses with the sweet slow-cooked vegetables to make a scrumptious dish. You can use other vegetables such as asparagus, peas or green beans, as well as different pulses such as chickpeas, cannellini or kidney beans. If bitterness is required, add some form of cabbage such as cavolo nero.

serves 4

3 tablespoons olive oil
140g (5oz) diced pancetta
1 onion, diced
2 carrots, peeled and diced
2 sticks of celery
1 clove of garlic
1 medium potato, peeled
2 courgettes
400g can chopped tomatoes
1 large sprig of basil
piece of Parmesan cheese rind
freshly ground black pepper
410g can borlotti beans, drained and rinsed
freshly grated Parmesan cheese to taste

1 The key to successfully cooking this recipe is to prepare each vegetable while the preceding one is cooking. Try to ensure that all the vegetables are roughly diced to the same size. Begin by pouring the oil into a large saucepan and set over a medium-low heat. Add the pancetta and, while it is frying, dice the onion. Once the pancetta has released much of its fat and is beginning to colour, stir in the onion and set to work on the carrots.

2 Fry the onion until meltingly soft, then add the diced carrots. Leave to cook while you dice the celery and add it to the pan, then finely chop the garlic and add that to the pan too. Dice the potato and stir it into the pan, then do the same with the courgettes. Gently fry. Cook the courgette for about 2 minutes, then stir in the chopped tomatoes. Fill the tomato tin with water twice and pour it into the soup. Add the basil, Parmesan rind and freshly ground black pepper. Don't salt at this stage unless you are not using the Parmesan rind.

3 Increase the heat and bring to the boil, before lowering it again so that the soup gently bubbles, uncovered, for 2 hours. As it cooks it will thicken. When there are 20 minutes left before the end of the cooking time, season to taste and add the beans. You will need to add a little extra water to taste. Simmer until hot, then serve piping hot with extra grated Parmesan and lots of crusty bread. This soup tastes even better the following day.

salads

The art of making a good salad lies in the careful balancing of taste, texture and colour. A few grains of salt are often added at the end, like the magician's powder, to create an explosion of taste, yet for the consummate cook salty ingredients play a more integral role. The key is to start with the texture of your salty ingredient. Soft unctuous ingredients such as smoked trout, marinated kipper fillet and creamy cheeses need to be contrasted with slightly firmer succulent foods such as chicory, cucumber or cooked new potatoes. Conversely, firmer-textured salty foods such as shaved Parmesan, feta cheese or the crisp, juicy stems of samphire need softer-textured ingredients such as cooked asparagus, tomatoes, roasted peppers or salad leaves.

Bearing this in mind, begin assembling a delicious balance of sweet, sour and bitter ingredients to complement your chosen salty food. Sourness will bring out any intrinsic sweetness in an ingredient, but will also emphasize its saltiness. It stimulates the appetite. Bitterness will also increase the saltiness, but in moderation can add a tempting, sophisticated note. Olive oil, mustard or horseradish, for example, all make smoked salmon taste utterly alluring. Sweetness will lessen the saltiness but, without the aid of sourness or bitterness, will simply satiate the appetite.

Obviously, umami-tasting ingredients such as Parmesan, tomatoes or salted anchovies will add a further gustatory frisson to a salad. Take care, however, not to overload a dish with them, as they intensify our perception of salt and can easily ruin a good dish. Caesar salad, for example, benefits from a light hand.

avocado, black bean and bacon salad

Bacon is a useful way of introducing a more dominant salty note in a sweet, sour and bitter salad. Add the salty, umami allure of tomatoes and the last mouthful tastes as exciting as the first. Try bacon with other relatively sweet ingredients such as lentils, chickpeas, pasta or rice.

serves 2 as a main course

1 tablespoon white wine vinegar
1 clove of garlic, finely chopped
4 tablespoons extra virgin olive oil
salt and freshly ground black pepper
1 small red chilli, or to taste, finely chopped
425g can black beans, drained and rinsed
1 red or yellow pepper, quartered and deseeded
170g (6oz) back bacon, trimmed
1 ripe avocado
250g (9oz) baby plum tomatoes, peeled and quartered
a large handful of fresh coriander leaves, roughly chopped

1 In a salad bowl, whisk together the vinegar, garlic and 3 tablespoons of olive oil. Season to taste with salt, pepper and fresh chilli. Mix in the beans.

2 Arrange the pepper skin-side-up, under the grill. Cook until the skin blackens and blisters, then remove to a bowl and cover. Once cool, peel, dice and mix into the beans. Meanwhile, cut the bacon into medium-sized squares and fry briskly in a tablespoon of oil until crisp. Then tip, oil and all, into the beans. Finally, halve, peel and stone the avocado. Cut into dice and mix into the salad with the quartered tomatoes and chopped coriander. Adjust the seasoning if necessary and serve immediately.

goat's cheese, beetroot and samphire salad

In this recipe, the two salty but texturally contrasting ingredients of creamy goat's cheese and crisp samphire resonate with one another. The sweet beetroot softens their saltiness, while the tart vinaigrette and slightly bitter leaves transform this salad into a sophisticated and tempting dish. Try combining other salty ingredients, such as bacon and blue cheese or smoked salmon and capers, in salads.

serves 6

24 baby beetroots
1 small clove of garlic, finely chopped
1 tablespoon white wine vinegar
4 tablespoons walnut oil
salt and freshly ground black pepper
170g (6oz) fresh samphire, rinsed and trimmed of any woody stems
6 handfuls of mixed salad leaves
6 x 55g (2oz) small fresh goat's cheeses, such as Crottin de Chavignol

1 If using raw beetroot, trim the leaves to within 2.5cm (1-inch) of the root and scrub clean. Put the beetroot in a saucepan, liberally cover with cold water and set over a medium heat. Bring to the boil and cook until the beetroot are tender and peel easily – they should take about 30 minutes. Drain and set aside. Once the beetroot are cool enough to handle, don a pair of rubber gloves (to avoid pink hands), peel away their skins and snip off their roots. Halve or quarter each beetroot and place in a small bowl.

2 Whisk together the garlic, vinegar and 3 tablespoons walnut oil. Season to taste and dress the beetroot with a third of the vinaigrette.

3 Drop the samphire into a pan of boiling water and cook for a few seconds. Drain immediately, and cool under the cold tap. Gently pat dry in kitchen paper and place in a mixing bowl with the salad leaves.

4 Preheat the grill to medium-high. Place the cheeses on an oiled baking sheet and drizzle each with a little walnut oil. Grill for 3–4 minutes, or until they are flecked golden. Dress the salad leaves with the remaining vinaigrette. Arrange in a loose circle on 6 serving plates. Slip the dressed beetroot in among the leaves. Finally, add the hot cheese and serve immediately with good wholemeal or walnut bread.

oriental coleslaw

Soy sauce is a useful way of adding umami to a salad. Mix it with sour vinegar, sweet honey and bitter sesame oil and you have a dressing that lessens the bitterness of the cabbage and enhances the sweetness of the carrots.

serves 6

1 tablespoon Kikkoman soy sauce
½ tablespoon honey
½ tablespoon finely diced fresh ginger
1 clove of garlic, finely chopped
1 tablespoon white wine vinegar
2 tablespoons toasted sesame oil
1 tablespoon olive oil
½ small red cabbage, finely sliced
6 spring onions, trimmed and sliced
2 carrots, peeled and roughly grated
½ lime
a handful of fresh coriander leaves

1 Whisk together the soy sauce, honey, ginger, garlic, white wine vinegar, sesame oil and olive oil. Set aside.

2 Put the sliced cabbage in a large mixing bowl with the spring onions and grated carrots. Toss in the dressing and chill until needed, then squeeze over the lime juice, remix and serve scattered with coriander leaves.

caesar salad

No doubt the popularity of Caesar salad is partly due to the fact that salted anchovies and Parmesan have a strong savoury, umami taste. Combine this with sour lemon juice, and you have a refreshing, exciting salad. Remember that raw or partly cooked eggs can carry a risk of salmonella.

serves 4

6 tablespoons extra virgin olive oil
2 cloves of garlic, halved, plus 2, finely sliced
3 slices good white bread, crusted and cubed
salt and freshly ground black pepper
8 salted anchovy fillets, drained
3 tablespoons milk
4 plump cos lettuce, hearts separated and tough outer leaves discarded
4 teaspoons lemon juice
1 teaspoon Worcestershire sauce
1 medium egg, at room temperature
40g (1½oz) Parmesan cheese, finely grated

1 Preheat the oven to 180°C (350°F) gas mark 4. Put 2 tablespoons of oil and the halved garlic in a small pan over a low heat. Once hot, remove and leave to infuse for 10 minutes. Strain the oil over the bread and mix. Salt, scatter on a baking sheet and bake for 12–15 minutes. Set aside. Marinate the sliced cloves in 4 tablespoons of oil for 2 hours, then strain. Rinse the anchovies and soak in milk for 20 minutes. Rinse, dry and cut into strips. Put in a bowl and add the lettuce.

2 Put the juice and Worcestershire sauce in a small bowl. Drop an egg into a pan of boiling water and cook for 1 minute, then break into the lemon juice before whisking in the garlic oil; it should form an emulsion. Season to taste and gently mix into the lettuce with the croûtons and Parmesan. Serve immediately.

marinades

Any marinade that contains a generous handful of salt will alter the taste and texture of whatever is marinated in it. The longer a food is left in the marinade, the firmer and more salty it will become as the salt extracts its moisture, including any bitter juices. Consequently, most foods are salted after they have been marinated. That said, salt-based marinades can create gorgeous salty foods, as the salt intensifies their underlying taste. In Japan, grilled fish is often lightly salted before cooking to extract moisture and odour, while some firm-textured white fish suitable for sashimi is bathed in the equivalent of a seawater brine to add succulence and enhance its sweetness. The danger, as always, lies in over-salting, as this hides any other tastes.

Other tastes and flavours can be incorporated into a salt marinade. Sugar is often mixed with salt to make a more subtle marinade that doubly enhances the sweetness of a food such as salmon gravadlax or spiced beef (see p.136). Sourness or bitterness can be added by rubbing a food with alcohol before marination. Spices and herbs can also be mixed into salt or brine to add bitterness or a subtle aroma.

grilled salted herring with mustard butter

The oiliness of herrings makes them ideal for the Japanese salting method. Compare salted with unsalted herrings. The former taste less 'fishy' yet more intense, with a hint of sweetness. This method works well with mackerel, salmon and sardines. For total sophistication, serve a slightly 'bitter' mustard butter or lemon wedges.

serves 6

6 herrings, trimmed, heads removed and gutted
fine sea salt
55g (2oz) softened butter
2 teaspoons Dijon mustard
1 teaspoon lemon juice
1 tablespoon finely chopped fresh parsley
freshly ground black pepper
1½ tablespoons olive oil
1 lemon, cut into 8 wedges

1 Run a knife down the fish tummies to their tails, then place, belly splayed open, on a board. Firmly press along their spines. Turn over and snip off their tails. Pull away the spines with the attached bones. Trim the fillets and, using tweezers, tweak out small bones. Hold a handful of salt 35cm (14-inches) away from a clean plastic tray and evenly sprinkle the surface with salt. Lay the fillets skin-side-down on the tray, then let the remaining salt sift on to the fish. Chill for 40 minutes.

2 Beat together the butter, mustard, lemon and parsley. Lightly season and spoon on to some wet greaseproof paper in the shape of a sausage. Wrap up and gently roll until it forms a smooth cylinder. Chill until needed.

3 Brush the fish with oil, season with pepper, then place, flesh-side-down, on a hot barbecue. Grill for 3 minutes, until seared, then turn and cook for 4 minutes, until the skin is crisp and golden. Cut the butter into rounds and put one on each fillet. Serve with lemon.

confit of duck salad

The origins of this recipe lie in preserving meat by salting it before cooking and sealing it in hot fat. Here the duck is salted relatively lightly, with a mixture of Chinese five-spice powder and sweet herbs, to bring out its inherent sweetness. Interestingly, duck contains 69mg of free glutamate per 100g, which means that you will also enhance its umami taste. The salad is a classic mixture of sweet, sour, bitter and salty, perfectly designed to further emphasize the salty-sweet-umami taste of the duck.

serves 6

confit of duck

115g (4oz) coarse Maldon sea salt
freshly ground black pepper
1 teaspoon Chinese five-spice powder
5 fresh bay leaves
1 head of garlic, halved, plus 1 clove
of garlic, sliced
8 duck legs or breasts
1kg (2lb 3oz) duck or goose fat

salad

1 cucumber, finely sliced
1 bunch of baby spring onions, trimmed
1 curly endive heart, leaves separated
and trimmed
2 red chicory, leaves separated
1½ tablespoons good sherry vinegar
5 tablespoons extra virgin olive oil
a pinch of caster sugar

1 Mix together the salt, pepper, five-spice powder, 3 of the fresh bay leaves (ripped into small pieces) and the sliced garlic in a large bowl. Rub into the duck pieces and layer them, roughly coated, in the bowl. Cover with clingfilm, heavily weight and refrigerate for 24 hours.

2 The next day, melt the fat over a low heat with the 2 remaining bay leaves and the halved head of garlic. Rinse and pat dry the duck pieces, then immerse them in the warm fat. Simmer gently for 1½ hours. The duck is cooked when a wooden skewer can pass through the thickest part of the leg with no resistance. Remove from the fat and leave to cool. Once the fat is tepid, strain through a fine sieve into a clean saucepan, bring up to the boil and skim. Cool once again and re-strain.

3 Put the duck pieces into a clean container. Slowly cover with the fat, making sure that there are no air holes. Cover and store in the fridge for up to 3 days.

4 To serve, remove the duck from the fat and arrange the pieces in a dry frying pan. Fry briskly for about 16 minutes, until the fat turns crispy and golden and the meat is piping hot. Meanwhile, prepare the salad by mixing together the sliced cucumber, spring onions, curly endive and chicory in a large bowl. Whisk together the sherry vinegar and olive oil. Season to taste and add a liberal pinch of caster sugar. Once the duck is hot, remove and quickly shred the meat and fat. Mix into the salad, dress and arrange on 6 plates. Serve immediately.

sauces

Salty sauces are best employed when you want to enhance the savoury-sweet nature of a main dish. This is because they principally work by emphasizing any inherent sweetness in the food, which in turn counteracts any bitterness. A salty-bitter-sweet anchovy mayonnaise, for example, will make rare beef taste sweeter, partly by negating the bitter taste of its blood. However, when bitterness or sourness predominate, saltiness further enhances them. In reality, it's highly unlikely that you would ever want to serve a very bitter or sour food, let alone exaggerate it with a salty sauce, but there are occasions when it is worth playing with a subtly sweet bitterness. Thus, cauliflower cheese tastes wonderful because the bitter-sweet nature of the cauliflower is enhanced by the sophisticated blend of sweet milk, bitter-salty mustard and salty cheese.

As you might expect, umami sauces make their accompaniments taste delicious. Think of how scrumptious roast potatoes taste with gravy. This is because umami appears to make food taste more savoury and sweet. It also lessens sourness and bitterness. The latter can be tested by eating aubergine or asparagus tempura (see p.188), which becomes amazingly sweet when dunked in a soy sauce dip.

broad beans and bacon tossed with tagliatelle

Bacon has always been a natural accompaniment to broad beans. Its salty nature brings out their sweetness. Here, this salty-sweet combination has been made more tantalizing by the addition of bitter notes in the olive oil and lemon zest, thereby complementing the bitterness of the beans and enlivening the relatively bland sweetness of the pasta.

serves 2

115g (4oz) shelled young broad beans
115g (4oz) dried egg tagliatelle
a pinch of sea salt
3 tablespoons extra virgin olive oil
140g (5oz) pancetta or streaky bacon, diced
1 fat clove of garlic, finely diced
1 bunch of spring onions, finely sliced
1 lemon, finely grated
a handful of fresh basil leaves, finely sliced
freshly ground black pepper

1 Bring a small pan of water to the boil. Add the beans and cook for 4 minutes until tender. Drain and set to one side.

2 Cook the pasta in a large pan of boiling salted water. Check the packet for cooking times, as each brand varies surprisingly. Drain once cooked.

3 Heat the olive oil in a frying pan and fry the diced pancetta until it is just beginning to turn crispy. Stir in the garlic and spring onions. Continue to cook for 1 minute, then mix in the beans and lemon zest. As soon as they are hot, add the cooked tagliatelle and the basil, with olive oil to taste and lots of freshly ground black pepper. Serve immediately.

buckwheat noodles with soy-honey dressing

A careful juxtaposition of umami soy sauce with umami nori enhances the sweetness in the noodles, tofu and onions. They become irresistible with a hint of sweet honey, sour lemon and bitter sesame oil.

serves 2

2 teaspoons honey
2 teaspoons finely chopped fresh ginger
½ teaspoon chilli flakes
2 tablespoons soy sauce
1 tablespoon lemon juice
3 tablespoons toasted sesame oil
6 spring onions, finely sliced
200g (7oz) tofu, drained and diced
7.5g (¼oz) toasted nori
170g (6oz) Japanese buckwheat noodles

1 Put the honey, ginger, chilli and soy sauce in a small saucepan. Set over a low heat, swirling occasionally until the honey has melted. Simmer for 2 minutes, then cool. Once cold, whisk in the lemon juice and oil.

2 When ready, put the onions and tofu in a bowl. Add the dressing. Snip the nori into small pieces and scatter on top. Drop the noodles in a pan of unsalted boiling water, return to the boil and cook for 4–5 minutes, until *al dente*. Cool under the tap. Shake the noodles as dry as you can, mix into the tofu and serve.

roast lamb with samphire sauce

If you combine delicate, salty samphire with moreish umami lamb stock you will create a tantalizing dish. Turn to the chicken stock recipe on p.202 and follow the instructions to adapt it to lamb stock.

serves 2

285ml (½ pint) reduced lamb stock (see method)
140ml (¼ pint) dry Vermouth
4 French-trimmed racks of lamb
1 clove of garlic, very finely chopped
2 tablespoons olive oil
salt and freshly ground black pepper
115g (4oz) cold butter, diced
200g (7oz) fresh samphire, rinsed and trimmed of any woody stems

1 Preheat the oven to 180°C (350°F) gas mark 4. Pour plenty of unreduced lamb stock into a wide saucepan and boil vigorously until it has a good flavour. Pour the Vermouth into a small saucepan and boil until it reduces to 3 tablespoons, then mix in 285ml (½ pint) of lamb stock.

2 Place the lamb in a roasting pan and rub with garlic and oil. Season lightly. Per 450g (1lb) roast for 25 minutes (rare), 30 minutes (medium-rare) or 40 minutes (well done), using 1 rack to calculate the time. Allow the meat to rest while you finish the sauce.

3 Return the Vermouth stock to a simmer and whisk in the butter, a little at a time. Do not reboil. Drop the samphire into boiling unsalted water for a few seconds, drain well and add to the sauce. Carve the lamb into thick slices and serve immediately.

lamb burgers with roasted tomato relish

The incredible umami-sour-sweet-bitter-salty nature of tomatoes, makes them perfect for sauces as each element acts upon the accompaniment, regardless of whether it is fish-, meat-, fowl-, dairy- or grain-based. There are many different recipes, but here the tomatoes are roasted first to concentrate their taste. Try eating the lamb burgers with and without the relish.

serves 4

relish

450g (1lb) baby plum tomatoes
1 medium red onion, finely diced
1 fat clove of garlic, finely chopped
3 tablespoons olive oil
salt and freshly ground black pepper

lamb burgers

3 tablespoons olive oil
1 onion, finely diced
1 clove of garlic, finely diced
2 lemons, finely grated
4 tablespoons finely chopped fresh parsley
1 teaspoon finely chopped fresh thyme
½ teaspoon finely chopped fresh tarragon
500g (1lb 2oz) minced lamb

1 Preheat the oven to 180°C (350°F) gas mark 4. Mix the tomatoes on a baking tray with the red onion, garlic and olive oil and roast for 45 minutes, or until soft and gooey. Then remove and, once cool, squeeze the tomato flesh out of the skins into a bowl. Discard the skins and scrape the onion, garlic, tomato pulp and juices into the bowl and mix. Season to taste and serve at room temperature.

2 Meanwhile, make the burgers. Heat 2 tablespoons of oil in a small frying pan and gently fry the onion and garlic until very soft. Tip into a bowl and mix in the lemon zest, chopped herbs, minced lamb, salt and pepper. Test the seasoning by frying off a small meat patty. Once you are happy, divide the mixture equally into 4 burgers, neatly patting them into shape with a palette knife. Transfer to a plate lined with greaseproof paper, cover with a further sheet and chill until needed.

3 Preheat an oven-top grill-pan (or barbecue) over a medium-high heat. When ready, brush the burgers with 1 tablespoon of oil and grill for about 5 minutes per side. Serve with the tomato relish, chips or sauté potatoes and a salad.

savoury dishes

In Western society the very nature of a savoury dish ensures that it contains umami or salt, regardless of whether it is a breakfast or supper dish. The dish relies upon subtle layerings of taste and flavour that slowly develop as you eat it, rather than the stark contrast of taste used between sauce and food. A truly great dish will continue to excite from start to finish of every mouthful. Thus, in a simple chicken and mushroom pie, umami chicken stock can be complemented by salty bacon before both enhance the sweet nature of the sautéed onions, chicken and pastry. The delicate bitterness of the mushrooms can be softened by the umami and re-enlivened by the sour note of wine.

In practical terms, only small quantities of salty ingredients should be used in savoury dishes, or they can become inedible. It is hard to rectify over-salting. Dilution is the cure, but unfortunately a little salt goes a long way and it is not usually worth throwing good food after bad. If you do opt for dilution, use a relatively sweet food such as cream and never add stock, as its umami taste enhances your perception of salt. Sourness can also help, as it brings out innate sweetness, which will counteract the excess salt.

chilli cheese omelette

The addition of the salty-umami Parmesan and salt in this recipe enhances the sweetness of the butter, eggs and sautéed onions. It's amazing how sweet this dish makes buttered toast taste.

serves 1

15g (½oz) butter
½ small onion, diced
½ Thai green chilli (or to taste), finely diced
¼ teaspoon finely chopped fresh ginger
½ small clove of garlic, finely chopped
2 medium eggs
1 tablespoon roughly chopped fresh coriander leaves
salt and freshly ground black pepper
1 tablespoon Parmesan cheese, finely grated

1 Place an 18cm (7 inch) omelette pan over a low heat. Melt the butter and gently fry the onion, chilli, ginger and garlic for 5–6 minutes, or until soft.

2 Roughly beat the eggs with a fork. Add the coriander, salt and pepper. Increase the heat to medium-high and pour the eggs into the pan. Draw a wooden spoon through the eggs, towards the centre of the pan, letting the liquid egg refill the channels. As soon as the omelette shows the first sign of setting, sprinkle on the Parmesan. Once it begins to set, but is still soft, tilt the pan. Using a spatula, flip over one edge. Once the omelette is cooked to your liking, slide it on to the plate and serve with lots of hot buttered toast.

special stir-fried rice

Salt and umami are again mixed together in this recipe via the bacon and soy sauce. As a result, the other ingredients taste sweet and savoury, to the satisfaction of the eater. This is one of my favourite supper recipes.

serves 2

2 eggs, beaten with 2 teaspoons toasted sesame oil
pinch of salt
4 tablespoons sunflower oil
3 fine slices of fresh ginger
200g (7oz) smoked back bacon, cut into pea-sized dice
55g (2oz) frozen petit pois
115g (4oz) cooked and peeled prawns
55g (2oz) button mushrooms, cut into pea-sized dice
1 tablespoon soy sauce
1 tablespoon saké
425g (15oz) freshly cooked rice (200g/7oz uncooked rice yields this weight)
3 spring onions, finely sliced

1 Season the eggs and oil with a tiny pinch of salt. Place 2 tablespoons sunflower oil and the sliced ginger in a large non-stick frying pan and set over a medium heat. Once the ginger begins to sizzle and darken, remove from the pan and discard, then add the bacon. Stir-fry for 2 minutes, until it starts to crisp, then add the peas, prawns and mushrooms. Stir-fry for a further minute then add the soy sauce and saké. Allow it to bubble up, then tip the mixture into a bowl and set aside.

2 Wipe the frying pan clean and return it to the heat with 2 tablespoons sunflower oil. Once the oil is hot, add the eggs and lightly scramble them before stirring in the cooked rice. Keep stirring until it is piping hot, then mix in the bacon mixture and spring onions. Serve as soon as it is hot.

crispy parmesan-coated aubergine

As Parmesan contains plenty of umami it will lessen the bitterness of the aubergine. This dish can be accompanied by a tomato and basil sauce (see below) and a rocket salad.

serves 6

85g (3oz) Parmesan cheese, finely grated
generous pinch of cayenne pepper
85g (3oz) fresh white breadcrumbs
4 tablespoons plain flour, seasoned
2 medium eggs, beaten
2 large aubergines, cut into medium thick rounds
olive oil for frying
565ml (1 pint) tomato and basil sauce (see p.79)

1 Mix the Parmesan, cayenne and breadcrumbs in a bowl. Put the seasoned flour in another bowl and the beaten eggs in a third bowl. Coat the sliced aubergines by lightly dusting, one slice at a time, in flour, before dipping into the egg and pressing into the cheesy breadcrumbs. Set aside in a single layer.

2 Heat 5mm (¼ inch) olive oil in a large non-stick frying pan. As soon as it is hot, add a layer of breadcrumbed aubergine and fry over a medium heat for 2–3 minutes. Once golden, flip over and fry for a further 2–3 minutes, then remove and drain on kitchen paper. Repeat until all the aubergine is cooked, adding oil as necessary. Serve warm with the tomato sauce.

squid and prawn risotto

Similar tastes can be layered one upon another, as in this recipe, where the umami stock is invigorated by the savoury-sourness of the tomatoes and wine, all of which enhance the sweet nature of the other ingredients. The saffron and olive oil add a subtle bitter note, just to make it all the more sophisticated. This concept can be applied to stews and ragouts as well.

serves 2

225g (8oz) raw tiger prawns, in their shells
5 tablespoons olive oil
800ml (28fl oz) chicken stock
a pinch of saffron threads
225g (8oz) cleaned squid
1 onion, finely chopped
1 clove of garlic, finely chopped
200g (7oz) ripe tomatoes
185g (6½oz) Calasparra or risotto rice
3 tablespoons dry Vermouth
1 bay leaf
55g (2oz) frozen petit pois

1 Peel the prawns, saving the shells. Heat 1 tablespoon of olive oil in a small saucepan and add the prawn shells. Fry briskly until they turn pink. Add the chicken stock and bring up to the boil. Meanwhile, grind the saffron threads under a teaspoon, then add to the stock and reduce the heat to a simmer. Leave to cook and reduce slightly while you continue with the recipe.

2 Finish cleaning the prawns by cutting down the length of their backs and pulling away their digestive threads, if they are black or brown. Rinse the prawns, then pat dry and set aside. Rinse the squid and pat dry before cutting their bodies into rings.

3 Set a saucepan over a high heat. Add 2 tablespoons of olive oil and briskly fry the prawns until just pink. Remove with a slotted spoon and set aside. Stir-fry the squid until it turns opaque – it will only take a minute (it should be half-cooked). Add to the prawns, leaving as much of the oil as possible in the saucepan. Lower the temperature, add a further 2 tablespoons of olive oil and stir in the onion and garlic. Fry until soft.

4 To peel the tomatoes, cut a cross in the base of each and cover with boiling water for 2 minutes. Drain, peel and chop. Once the onion is soft, add the tomatoes and fry gently for 4 minutes to form a thick purée. Stir in the rice and fry for a further 3 minutes, stirring regularly. Add the Vermouth and bay leaf and cook until the liquid has almost evaporated. Strain the hot stock and add 600ml (a generous pint). Add the peas and adjust the seasoning. Bring to the boil, cover and set over a low heat, stirring occasionally, until the rice is *al dente*. Finally, mix in the prawns and squid with their juices, cover and turn off the heat. Leave to heat through for 2 minutes, then serve.

pizza

I suspect that one reason why pizza tastes so good is that it has a satisfying mix of sweet, sour, salty, bitter and umami tastes: sweet from the dough and mozzarella; umami, sour, salty and sweet from the tomato sauce; salty from the meat; bitter and salty from the olives; and umami and salty from the Parmesan. You can, of course, vary the topping to taste. Try roasted peppers, Parma ham or baby artichoke hearts.

serves 2 as a main course

pizza dough

225g (8oz) plain flour
½ teaspoon salt
½ teaspoon easy-blend dried yeast
85ml (3fl oz) milk
1 tablespoon olive oil, plus extra for bowl

topping

1 small onion, finely sliced
2 tablespoons olive oil
1 clove of garlic, finely diced
a pinch of dried chilli flakes (optional)
255g (9oz) ripe tomatoes
2 sprigs of basil
salt and freshly ground black pepper
70g (2½oz) finely sliced chorizo
5 fat olives, stoned and quartered
1 mozzarella cheese, sliced
20g (¾oz) Parmesan cheese, finely grated

1 Sift the flour and salt into a mixing bowl. Stir in the yeast, followed by the milk and 85ml (3fl oz) tepid water. Using your hands, mix together until it forms a soft, pliant dough. Turn out and knead thoroughly for 5 minutes, or until it feels silky smooth. Roughly flatten it, and make a few indentations with your fingertips. Pour over 1 tablespoon olive oil and fold the dough over it, carefully kneading until the oil is absorbed. It will be very squelchy initially.

2 Shape into a ball, lightly oil and return to a large bowl. Cover with clingfilm and leave in a warm place for 2 hours, or until the dough has doubled in size.

3 Meanwhile, make the topping. Gently fry the onion in the olive oil in a small saucepan for about 5 minutes, then add the garlic and chilli flakes and continue to fry for 2–3 minutes. Peel the tomatoes by covering with boiling water for 1–2 minutes, then stripping away their skins. Roughly chop their flesh and add, with the basil, to the softened onions. Continue to cook until they form a thick, almost dry, purée, then remove the basil and season to taste, remembering that both the chorizo and Parmesan are salty.

4 Place a heavy baking sheet in the oven and preheat to its highest setting. Knock back the dough and roll out to a round about 30cm (12 inches) in diameter. Using a rolling pin, lift the dough on to the hot baking sheet and quickly spread with the tomato paste. Top with the chorizo and olives, followed by the sliced mozzarella. Finally sprinkle with the Parmesan and place in the oven. Bake for between 10–15 minutes, depending on your oven. It is cooked when the cheese is melted and flecked gold and the crust looks crisp and golden.

chicken, mushroom and bacon pie

This is a sophisticated example of layering similar tastes. The umami chicken stock and salty bacon combine to enhance the sweetness of the sautéed vegetables, chicken and pastry, which are offset by the acidic wine and bitter lemon zest. Cream can be added, but it will dilute the savoury nature of the pie and make it taste slightly sweeter. This taste combination can be adapted to casseroles.

serves 4

You will need a 1.7 litre (3 pint) pie dish for this recipe
225g (8oz) chilled shortcrust pastry (see p.203)
170g (6oz) good streaky bacon, diced
4 tablespoons plain flour
salt and freshly ground black pepper
4 large chicken breasts, skinned and boned
2 tablespoons sunflower oil
1 medium onion, finely diced
1 clove of garlic, finely diced
4 carrots, peeled and cut into batons
200g (7oz) white button mushrooms
140ml (¼ pint) dry Vermouth
565ml (1 pint) good chicken stock (see p.202)
3 strips finely pared lemon peel
3 sprigs fresh parsley tied with 3 sprigs of fresh thyme and a bay leaf
3 tablespoons milk

1 Preheat the oven to 190°C (375°F) gas mark 5. Roll out the pastry to the same shape as your pie dish, but a little larger. Cut a ribbon from around the edge of the pastry and press it firmly on to the rim of the pie dish. Chill the pastry while you make the filling.

2 Preheat a sauté pan over a medium heat and add the bacon. As its fat melts, stir-fry until crisp, then remove with a slotted spoon, leaving the fat in the pan.

3 Season the flour. Cut the chicken into 2.5cm (1-inch) chunks. Dust in some of the flour and fry in single-layer batches in the pan. Cook briskly until lightly coloured, adding extra oil to the sauté pan as necessary. Set aside with the bacon.

4 Add another tablespoon of oil to the pan and gently fry the onion, garlic and carrots until soft, then stir in the mushrooms. As soon as they begin to colour, mix in the remaining seasoned flour and cook for a couple of minutes before adding the Vermouth. Boil vigorously until the liquid has almost evaporated, then stir in the stock, peel and herbs. Return to the boil. Mix in the bacon and chicken and adjust the seasoning to taste.

5 Tip into the pie dish and squash a pie funnel (if you have one) into the middle. Brush the pastry ribbon with some milk. Loosely roll the pastry on to the rolling pin and lift on to the pie dish. Using a fork, firmly press around the rim so that the layers of pastry are sealed together. Trim off the excess pastry. Prick the lid with a knife and brush with the milk.

6 Place in the centre of the oven and turn the heat down to 180°C (350°F) gas mark 4. Bake for 45 minutes, or until the pastry is crisp and golden.

puddings and cakes

Salt is not a taste that is commonly associated with puddings and cakes, yet it has a useful role in sweet food. Salt lessens the intensity of sweetness, yet at the same time imbues the dish with a satisfyingly complex depth, which makes the eater feel replete. A simple way to test this is to try meringue made with and without a pinch of salt. When a recipe has several sweet ingredients, for example a buttery pound cake, the salt seems to lessen the innate sweetness while at the same time enhancing the individual tastes of butter, flour, eggs and sugar. Similarly, it will highlight other flavourings such as spices or essences. Take care not to add extra salt in other forms. Salted butter, for example, can replace salt in cakes, biscuits and pastry.

Sweet-saltiness can be combined with bitterness. The effect is two-fold: the dish loses its fresh intensity because bitterness complicates the tastes, but it also closes the appetite because bitterness satisfies when combined with sweetness. Umami is not, so far as I am aware, used much in puddings, presumably because it has a savoury taste. One exception is seaweed. The Bretons make seaweed chocolates, in which seaweed is flecked through the soft, bitter-sweet chocolate ganache filling. They taste fantastic and moreish. The appetizing nature of the umami seems to counteract the satisfying nature of bitter-sweet.

coconut black rice pudding

Thai cooking commonly mixes salt and sweet tastes in puddings, which has the effect of satisfying the eater at the end of a meal. This works particularly well with coconut milk and sugar. Here, fresh mango adds a sweet-sour note that refreshes the palate from the intense sweet-salty nature of the coconut rice, while at the same time sharpening the perception of these two tastes.

serves 4

200g (7oz) Oriental black rice
sea salt
5 tablespoons light brown muscovado sugar
300ml (10½fl oz) canned coconut milk
1 mango, peeled

1 Wash the rice until the water runs clear. Tip into a saucepan and add 450ml (16fl oz) of water. Bring to the boil, stir once, cover and reduce the heat to a low simmer. Cook for 30-35 minutes, or until the rice is *al dente*. Stir in 1 teaspoon sea salt with 3 tablespoons of muscovado sugar, or to taste. Divide the cooked rice between 4 x 150ml (5fl oz) well-oiled dariole moulds. Press down, cover lightly with clingfilm, and weight with 4 more moulds filled with water. Leave for 10 minutes.

2 Put the coconut milk, a pinch of salt and 2 tablespoons of muscovado sugar into a small saucepan. Set over a low heat and simmer until it has slightly thickened. Cut the mango flesh away from its stone in 4 segments. Finely slice each segment lengthways.

3 Gently turn the rice out on to 4 plates, add the milk and garnish with the mango. Serve warm or cold.

floating islands

Poached meringue islands, floating in a sea of sweet custard, perfectly illustrate how salt draws out the different sweet tastes of all the ingredients. This recipe may look long, but each part can be made separately in advance. The islands keep well for a day or two in their custard. As salt increases the whipping time and decreases the foam's stability in egg whites, it is added near the end of whipping. It also increases the speed of coagulation with the egg yolks in the custard.

serves 6

for the custard

565ml (1 pint) custard (see p.201 but omit the vanilla pod)
2 teaspoons distilled orange flower water

islands

565ml (1 pint) milk
4 medium egg whites
115g (4oz) caster sugar
a pinch of salt

1 As instructed on p.201, pour the warm vanilla-less custard into the bowl of chilled cream and stir until it is tepid. Then stir in the orange flower water, cover and chill until needed.

2 Prepare the islands by pouring the milk and 565ml (1 pint) water into a wide shallow saucepan. Bring to a very gentle simmer, so that only the occasional bubble floats up.

3 Place the egg whites in a large, clean, dry bowl and whisk until they form soft peaks. Slowly add the sugar, whisking all the time, until they form a stiff, glossy meringue. Finally whisk in the salt.

4 Using 2 dessertspoons, shape the meringue into a lozenge and drop into the barely simmering liquid. Repeat until you have 4 islands poaching in the milky water. Cook for 1 minute, then gently flip over and cook for another minute. Do not overcook or they will disintegrate.

5 Gently lift the cooked meringues out with a slotted spoon and lay them on a cooling rack to drain. Continue to cook the remaining mixture. Once finished, leave the islands to drip for 30 minutes, so that they will not dilute the custard. Strain the custard into a serving dish and float the meringues on it. Cover and chill until needed.

preserves

Salt is widely used in preserves as a means of extracting moisture and inhibiting the growth of bacteria. Some foods, such as gherkins and onions, are salted before being rinsed and preserved in vinegar; while other foods, such as lemons, cabbages and oily fish, are preserved in either dry salt or in a salty brine. In all cases, the texture becomes firmer as the moisture is extracted. A by-product of salting is that it removes any bitter juices from a food; thus cucumbers or cauliflower will taste sweeter if they are salted before pickling.

All salted food develops an intense taste that is predominately salty but in some cases, such as with anchovies, may also be umami. To fully appreciate the taste of salted foods, some of the excess salt is usually removed by rinsing or soaking before use. The food is then used as a salty, sour and/or bitter element in a recipe.

salted lemons

Salting lemons reduces the bitterness in their pith and peel, making them taste seductively sour and salty with a bitter note which works well with relatively bland, sweet foods such as lamb or chicken. Like all salted foods, only a small amount is needed to enhance a recipe. Ideally, buy organic or unwaxed lemons for this wonderful Claudia Roden recipe, which I've adapted from her lovely book *Tamarind and Saffron*.

makes 4 lemons

4 thick-skinned lemons
4–5 juicy lemons
4 tablespoons coarse sea salt

1 Preheat the oven to 140°C (275°F) gas mark 1. To sterilize your pickle or Kilner jar, wash in soapy water, rinse, and then put them in the oven until dry.

2 Wash the 4 thick-skinned lemons thoroughly, then pat dry and cut each lemon into quarters, but not right through, so that the pieces are still attached at the stem end. Stuff each lemon with plenty of salt and layer into the sterilized jar, pressing firmly down as you do so. Close the jar and leave for 3–4 days. The lemons will have softened and released some of their juice.

3 Juice the 4–5 juicy lemons. Press the salted lemons down and add enough juice to cover them. Leave for a minimum of a month. Rinse off the salt before using.

salt notes

Sea salt can be given a more complex flavour by mixing in finely chopped fresh thyme leaves, crushed chilli flakes or roughly ground black pepper before use. This works particularly well on relatively sweet fried foods, for example home-made root vegetable crisps or savoury fritters such as squid or onion.

Freshly grated Parmesan cheese adds an addictive umami, salty taste to everything from pasta to risotto. It can be sprinkled on to creamy gratins, pizza toppings and croûtons or mixed into quiches, soups and sauces, as well as pressed on to fish, chicken or veal escalopes.

A good home-made meat or fowl stock (see p.202) has a natural umami saltiness that will add a luscious depth to all manner of foods. If you want to intensify its meaty taste, roast the bones and vegetables before turning into stock.

If in need of an instant salty note for a salad, sauce or pizza topping, try adding preserved artichoke hearts, capers, olives or pickled gherkins as appropriate. If you are after a sophisticated taste, opt for ingredients that are also bitter, such as artichoke hearts, olives and gherkins.

Home-made or bought teriyaki sauce, brushed over pan-seared food, gives it a sweet-umami crust. Try with salmon, steak or boned chicken thighs. It's very easy to make, but you will need to find mirin (a sweet rice spirit, which is available from Asian grocers). Measure 7 tablespoons each of saké, mirin and naturally brewed dark soy sauce in a saucepan. Simmer for 2 minutes, cool and store chilled. To use, fry food until nearly cooked, then remove from the pan. Add the sauce and cook until it thickens slightly. Return the food and finish cooking, turning regularly, until thoroughly coated and the sauce is almost completely reduced.

A powerful umami kick can be given to sandwiches by adding a well-matured blue cheese such as roquefort, Dolcelatta or Stilton. Such cheeses will enhance the sweet taste of the bread, especially if combined with bitter watercress leaves and sweet slices of pear.

A classic tomato sauce is a useful way to add a savoury, salty element to a variety of dishes. To make 565ml (1 pint), gently fry 2 roughly chopped onions and 2 roughly chopped cloves of garlic in 5 tablespoons of olive oil until they are meltingly soft. Roughly chop 900g (2lb) of ripe tomatoes and stir into the onions with 3 strips of finely pared lemon peel and 3 sprigs of fresh basil and parsley. Season to taste and simmer gently until thick and flavoursome. Remove the lemon peel, purée, strain and serve. A small piece of Parma ham or a little fresh chilli cooked with the onions will imbue the sauce with a salty depth and some heat, respectively.

Salted anchovies can be added to butters or mayonnaise to make a wonderful salty-sweet-tasting sauce. For the former, rinse 3 anchovies of any excess salt or oil and soak in 3 tablespoons milk for 20 minutes. Rinse again and pat dry before finely chopping to a paste. Transfer to a small bowl and beat in about a teaspoon of lemon juice, followed by 55g (2oz) of softened butter and a couple of tablespoons of fresh parsley. Season to taste with black pepper and ground mace. This is particularly good on steak or grilled fish such as salmon, and on steamed vegetables such as cauliflower or green beans.

Smoked fish will imbue a recipe with a delicate salty taste, regardless of whether the fish is smoked haddock or salmon. Consequently they are often partnered with relatively sweet foods such as rice, cream, potato, butter, blinis or bread. Lemon juice naturally enhances their salty-sweet nature.

bitter

Bitterness is the most intriguing of the five tastes. To quote the scientist Bernd Lindemann in his article in *Nature*, 'bitter taste is unpleasant though bearable when weak, but repulsive when strong'. Bitterness acts as a warning against eating substances that can affect how the body functions – caffeine, nicotine and strychnine, for example, are all bitter. Babies differentiate between bitter and sweet tastes very early in life, and their dislike of the former protects them from accidentally poisoning themselves. Yet from the cook's perspective many bitter ingredients can add a fascinating complexity to the taste of food. Dress orange segments in a bitter-sweet caramel syrup, for example, and their fresh taste becomes surprisingly sophisticated.

The enjoyment of bitter food tends to develop with age. Few children like the bitterness of an unsweetened espresso, green cabbage or globe artichoke, although they might be persuaded to lick some black treacle or try some sweetened bitter chocolate. Even adults find it necessary to lessen bitterness in food. Normally a bitter ingredient is either diluted with liquid, as with tea or coffee, or it is prepared in a way that will remove some of its bitterness, such as the traditional methods of salting or blanching in boiling water. The former will extract bitter juices from gourds, aubergine and such like, while the latter dilutes the peppery bitter chemicals called glucosinolates in the leaves of watercress, cabbage et al. Since farmers have bred sweeter strains of vegetables over the centuries, these practices are becoming less necessary. Occasionally bitterness, like any other dominant taste, may need to be intensified, and this can be done by deep-frying or oven-drying. Thus, shredded deep-fried spring greens (Chinese seaweed) or dried Seville orange zest will taste deliciously bitter.

It is then a question of using the other tastes to enhance a bitter food. Sourness, for example, appears to lessen our perception of bitterness, making it taste fresher, just as saltiness and umami enhance any inherent sweetness in a bitter ingredient. Toss some Belgian endive in a few drops of lemon juice with a hint of salt and you will see what I mean. Some bitter ingredients, such as coffee or cocoa, have no natural sweetness and can taste unpleasant when combined with sour or salty ingredients. But sweeten these bitter ingredients, even add another bitter element such as orange or lemon zest, and the bitterness is softened into an alluring adult taste. Conversely, when bitterness is added to an intrinsically sweet dish, the dish becomes less cloying.

Importantly, bitterness also seems to influence our appetite, which makes it a useful adjunct when planning a meal. Add a touch of bitterness to a predominately salty-sour savoury recipe that has a hint of sweetness, such as hot and sour soup, and you will create an exciting yet satisfying dish. Mix bitterness with pure sweetness, for example, in a chocolate soufflé, and you can satiate hunger in a delectable way.

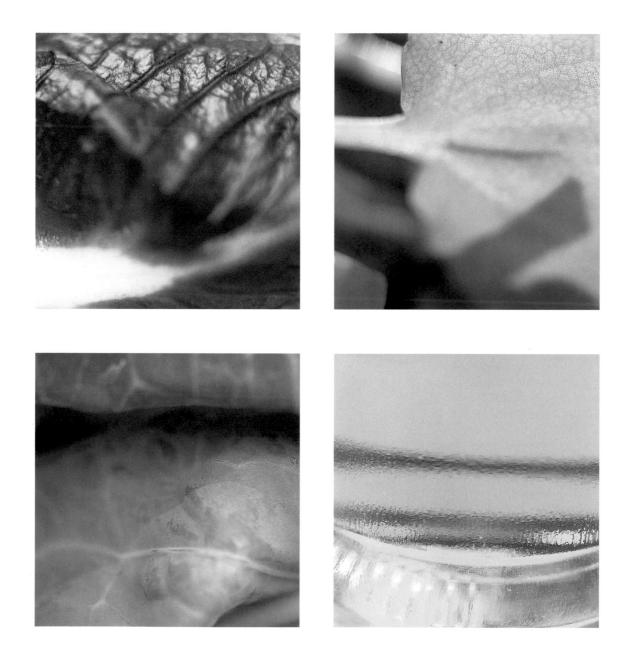

chicory

The name chicory frequently confuses cooks, as it can refer to several kinds of chicories *(Cichoirum intybus)* and endives *(Cichorium endivia)*. They are all closely related and relatively bitter. *C. intybus* includes all the deep red chicories and the white Belgian endive (witloof or chicory). *C. endivia* is divided between curly- and broad-leafed varieties, including curly endive (frisée), and escarole (batavia).

Blanching (growing in the dark) reduces chicory's natural bitterness. Accidentally expose a Belgian endive to daylight and it will turn green and bitter. Similarly, the dark green outer leaves of curly endive are more bitter than its pale heart. Sour ingredients such as citrus fruits or vinegar will make chicory taste sweeter, just as salty foods such as bacon or blue cheese will counterbalance its bitterness by enhancing its sweetness. Cooking also lessens its bitterness.

watercress

Scientists believe that many bitter plants, such as watercress *(Nasturtium officinale)*, developed bitter-tasting glucosinolates in their leaves to deter the likes of sheep or freshwater shrimps from munching them. Unfortunately for the plant, some such tastes can have the opposite effect on a committed gourmet like man. Watercress's slightly bitter, peppery taste stimulates our palate in the most delicious way, making watercress a useful addition to a wide variety of dishes. Raw or cooked, it adds a tantalizing bitter note to herbal butters, mayonnaise and cream-based sauces, as well as salads and sandwiches. It tastes particularly good with tart vinaigrettes, lemony roast chicken juices, bacon, soy sauce, sweet prawns, pears, olives and umami cheeses. If you wish to lessen watercress's bitterness, drop into boiling water for a few seconds, cool immediately and squeeze dry.

spring greens

Spring greens (collards in America) are a type of loose-hearted green cabbage which – like all members of the *Brassica* family, including watercress, mustard and rocket – contain chemicals called glucosinolates in their leaves. These chemicals imbue them with varying degrees of mustard-like bitterness, which is especially strong in the darker outer leaves. Over the centuries, this intrinsic bitterness has slowly diminished as sweeter varieties have been developed. It can be lessened further by dropping the greens into a pan of boiling water for a minute or two, or stir-frying them in a non-bitter oil such as sunflower oil for a few seconds. If, however, the greens are over-cooked or finely sliced and deep-fried (as for crispy Chinese seaweed), their bitterness will be increased. Salty ingredients such as soy sauce will bring out the sweetness of spring greens.

extra virgin olive oil

Anyone who has ever bitten into a freshly-picked olive will know that it tastes disgustingly bitter. Olives contain oleuropein, a bitter glucoside, in their watery, acidic sap. This glucoside is removed naturally when olive oil is made – after the olives have been crushed and pressed, the extracted liquid is spun centrifugally to separate the oil from the acidic, bitter water. Like wine, extra virgin olive oils vary enormously in taste according to the olive variety, growing conditions, ripeness and pressing methods. Greener (unripe) olives bring a greater bitterness to the final oil. At its best, as with some of the estate-bottled extra-virgin Tuscan olive oils, this bitterness is carefully balanced by grassy, peppery flavours. This inherent bitterness can be very useful to the cook. Its subtlety adds a tantalizing hint of sophistication to foods in dishes such as salads, sauces, sautés and grills.

bitter oranges

Bitter or sour oranges *(Citrus aurantium)*, such as Seville oranges, contain a bitter compound called neotresperidin which, along with their sour juice, gives them an intense orange taste, perfect for cooking. Small, rough-skinned and russetted, these oranges are a reminder of a time when taste came before beauty. They are mainly grown in Spain for the British market and appear in mid-January for three weeks.

The greatest bitterness is found in their pith and skin, which is why Seville oranges make such exquisite sweet preserves. However, their bitter aromatic skin also brings out the subtle sweetness of cakes and creamy puddings. This bitterness can be reduced by finely paring the skin from the pith and blanching in boiling water. It is intensified by drying in a cool oven instead of blanching. In either case, infuse into sweet-sour sauces to accompany meat or fish.

dark chocolate

In the wild, cocoa beans are guaranteed dispersal by the clever ploy of coating their bitter seeds (the beans) with a slippery, sweet pulp. Like coffee, cocoa beans contain bitter phenolic compounds. Butter-fingered monkeys drop the unappetizing beans while trying to eat the refreshing mucilaginous flesh between the hard pod and bitter seed. Chocolate producers limit this natural bitterness and develop flavour by briefly fermenting the freshly-picked pulp-coated seeds, as well as by roasting and blending the beans later. Nevertheless, dark chocolate and cocoa are essentially bitter substances that need sweetening and/or dilution to be palatable. A little chocolate will highlight other sweeter foods such as banana or pear, and complement bitter ingredients such as coffee or nuts. Certain flavourings, such as vanilla, will make chocolate seem sweeter.

coffee

The first Western impressions of coffee were not always favourable. Sir Thomas Herbert, encountering it in Persia in the 1620's, described coffee as 'a drink imitating that in the Stygian lake, black, thick and bitter'. Today, coffee beans mainly come from *Coffea arabica* and the less fine-flavoured *Coffea canephora* (robusta). Once roasted, ground and infused, myriad different aromatic molecules combine with protein, oil, tannins, sugar, starch, fibre, caffeine and bitter phenolic substances to imbue coffee with a wonderfully complex taste. Much, however, depends on its preparation. The finer coffee beans are ground, for example, the stronger and more bitter the drink. Similarly, the longer it is brewed, the more bitter and astringent it will become. Coffee adds a sophisticated bitterness to sweet puddings, particularly when combined with other bitter foods such as chocolate or nuts.

angostura bitters

Bitter-tasting foods have always been associated with both poison and medicine. Angostura aromatic bitters, for example, was originally created in the early 1820s as a medicine rather than a food. Dr Johann Siegert, a German physician working for General Bolivar in Venezuela, invented it to try to cure the terrible stomach disorders suffered by his soldiers in the liberation army. The resulting bitter concoction, made from 27 secret ingredients, including gentian root and orange zest, rapidly gained favour as a cure-all before being assimilated into cooking.

Trinidadians, in particular, excel at cooking with Angostura bitters, no doubt because it has been made there since around 1875. It is added as a seasoning to fresh fruit, splashed over ice-cream, stirred into bitter dark fruit cakes and rubbed into marinating meat and fish.

drinks

Diluted bitter drinks such as coffee, tea, chocolate, tonic water (quinine) and some alcoholic digestifs have long been popular. However, aside from tea and coffee, it is unusual to drink bitter drinks unsweetened. Thus, in the interests of culinary research, make a cup of black coffee or tea and savour its diluted bitter taste. Then try a Perrier pick-me-up so you can compare the stimulating effect of diluted bitterness with a hint of saltiness – Perrier water is naturally quite salty. Too much salt will intensify bitterness.

The brave can verify this by lightly salting a black coffee, but have a violet cream close by to take away the taste!

Sweetness makes bitterness palatable by giving the illusion of lessening it. This combination also satisfies the appetite, as a cup of cocoa or hot chocolate will prove. Some alcoholic bitter drinks are sweetened and soured, which creates a tantalizing, moreish taste. Perhaps for this reason, bitterness is frequently added to sweet-sour drinks, such as rum punch (p.127) or Champagne cocktail.

perfect cafetière coffee

A simple example of diluted bitterness. Methods for making coffee will differ according to whether you are using a cafetière, filter or espresso machine. If the water has been boiled or the coffee is brewed for too long, some of the coffee's aromatic oils are destroyed and the balance of flavour and bitterness is lost.

makes 1 mug

3 tablespoons medium coarsely ground coffee beans (these will vary in bitterness according to their origin, blend and roast)

1 Put a kettle of cold water on to boil. As soon as it comes up to boiling point, but before it reaches a full boil, turn off the heat. Swill hot water in the cafetière. Discard the water. Measure in the coffee. Add 300ml (11fl oz) hot water, stir once with a knife, and leave for 4 minutes. Push down the plunger. Serve immediately. If the coffee is too strong, dilute with hot water in the cup. If you wish to add milk, gently heat it in a pan (do not boil).

perrier pick-me-up

The combination of the salty mineral water and fruity bitters is very refreshing. Start with just a little bitters, then as you become used to its taste, increase the quantity so that you have a pink drink.

serves 1

2–3 ice cubes
2-3 shakes of Angostura bitters
Perrier mineral water, chilled

1 Put the ice cubes in a glass tumbler and splash with the Angostura bitters.

2 Fill the glass with Perrier water and serve.

cinnamon hot chocolate

Unlike cocoa, all chocolate is sweetened, but in this drink the bitterness is both diluted and sweetened by the milk and cream. Cinnamon also enhances sweet tastes.

serves 2

565ml (1 pint) full-fat milk
140ml (¼ pint) single cream
1 stick cinnamon, broken
115g (4oz) good dark chocolate, such as Valrhona, roughly grated

1 Pour the milk and cream into a saucepan. Add the cinnamon and set over a low heat. When very hot, but not boiling, whisk in the grated chocolate. Keep whisking until the chocolate has melted. Remove the cinnamon, pour into 2 deep bowls or cups and serve.

bitter orange liqueur

This is a good example of a bitter-sweet-sour drink. In theory it could also be made with lemons, although I have not tried it. It can be drunk on its own or used as a bitter orange flavouring in puddings.

makes 1.6 litres (2¾ pints)

8 organic Seville oranges
450g (1lb) caster sugar
1 litre (1¾ pints) good brandy

1 Wash the oranges. If not organic, give them a firm wipe with a soft cloth before drying. Finely pare the skin from the oranges, making sure that no white pith is attached to it.

2 Put the finely pared peel in a large bowl with the sugar and brandy. Squeeze the oranges and strain their juice into the brandy. Stir occasionally until the sugar has dissolved, then transfer to 2 sterilized containers (for instructions on how to sterilize see page 43) with air-tight lids. Leave in a cool, dark place for at least 2 months before use.

soups

Soups fall into three categories: smooth purées, broths filled with toothsome morsels, and intermediate chunky soups such as gazpacho. Mildly bitter ingredients can be used in any of these; however, for maximum effect, analyze the primary tastes in your soup. If, for example, the soup is made with a stock, the underlying taste will be umami. This flatters bitter ingredients such as courgette or asparagus, regardless of whether they are puréed into a smooth soup or dropped into a minestrone. Alternatively, the primary taste might be salty-sour, as with a chunky tomato-based soup, or a hot sour broth (see p.93). Curiously, in a salty-sour liquid bitter ingredients taste better if they retain their texture rather than being puréed. This allows the sourness to enhance sweetness in the bitter ingredient, something it can't do when homogenized. One exception is extra virgin olive oil, which will always add a subtle bitter note.

white bean soup with olive oil

The mild sweet taste of cannellini beans is enlivened by the classic combination of umami stock, sweet sautéed onions and lavish amounts of relatively bitter olive oil. The final coup is the Parmesan, which ensures that the taste buds are completely excited with a further seasoning of salt and umami.

serves 6–8

500g (1lb 2oz) dried cannellini beans
4 onions
4 cloves of garlic
1 stick of celery, cut into 3 pieces
1 bay leaf
3 sprigs of fresh parsley
5 tablespoons extra virgin olive oil
1 small sprig of fresh rosemary
1 litre (1¾ pints) good chicken stock
salt and freshly ground black pepper
finely grated Parmesan cheese to serve

1 Soak the beans overnight in plenty of cold water. The next day, drain and rinse them, then place in a saucepan with lots of water. Bring to the boil, skim off the foam and boil vigorously for 10 minutes. Halve 2 onions and add them, with 2 cloves of garlic, the celery, bay leaf and parsley, and gently boil for an hour, or until the beans are meltingly tender. Drain and remove the onion and herbs.

2 Finely slice the remaining onions. Heat the olive oil in a saucepan over a low heat. Add the onions, along with the remaining whole garlic cloves and the rosemary sprig. Gently fry for about 30 minutes, until meltingly soft and golden, then add the stock. Bring up to the boil, remove the rosemary and add the cooked beans. Adjust the seasoning to taste and simmer gently for 30 minutes. Serve with extra olive oil and lots of freshly grated Parmesan.

hot and sour prawn and spring green soup

The umami-sour broth makes both the sweet prawns and bitter greens taste sweeter. However, such a simple soup needs a good home-made chicken stock (see p.202 for a recipe).

serves 4

500g (2lb 3oz) whole raw tiger prawns
2 tablespoons sunflower oil
2 cloves of garlic, roughly chopped
2 shallots, roughly chopped
1 litre (1¾ pints) good chicken stock
4 stalks of lemon grass, cut into
2.5cm (1-inch) lengths
4 lime leaves
3 strips of finely pared lime peel
2 green chillies, finely sliced
12 canned straw mushrooms, drained and
halved, or a handful of fresh shiitake
mushrooms, ripped into chunks
55g (2oz) spring greens, roughly sliced
½ tablespoon fish sauce (nam pla)
2 limes, juiced
1 red chilli, finely sliced, optional
2 tablespoons fresh coriander leaves

1 Peel the prawns, keeping the heads and shells. Clean the prawns by running a knife down the length of their backs and removing the thin digestive cord. Wash, pat dry and chill until needed.

2 Heat the oil in a large saucepan over a medium-high heat. Add the garlic, shallots and prawn heads and shells and stir-fry briskly until they turn pink. Add the chicken stock, lemon grass, lime leaves, lime zest and green chillies. Bring to the boil, skim, cover and simmer for 20 minutes, then strain into a clean saucepan.

3 When you are ready to serve, bring the stock up to the boil and add the peeled prawns, mushrooms and spring greens. Simmer briskly for 2–3 minutes, or until the prawns are pink, then reduce the heat and mix in the fish sauce and lime juice. Transfer immediately to soup bowls, sprinkle with the red chilli and coriander leaves and serve.

salads

A touch of bitterness in a salad can make the difference between a mundane and a brilliant dish. Bitterness adds an extra dimension of taste that excites the taste buds, even if it is only present in the vinaigrette (both olive oil and mustard are bitter). However, salads become really interesting when you start to assemble them from bitter ingredients such as chicory, watercress or cabbage. If you feel that an ingredient is too bitter to eat raw, remember that it can always be blanched or grilled. Cauliflower and purple sprouting broccoli, for example, are often lightly boiled before they are added to salads, while radicchio and Belgian endive are sometimes grilled.

It is then a question of learning how to utilize an ingredient's intrinsic bitterness to best effect. Sour dressings, for example, will make bitter foods such as watercress taste amazingly fresh, while salty or umami ingredients such as capers or blue cheese will bring out any underlying sweetness. Sweet ingredients, such as avocado pear or crab meat, also enhance the sweetness of bitter ingredients. Surprisingly, combining bitter ingredients has the same effect: grilled courgette with curly endive, for instance, or watercress with chicory and olives. Such an exercise enables you to create a symphony of harmonious tastes that resonate with one another in a gorgeous way.

chicory, lemon and caper salad with smoked salmon

The sour lemon juice and crème fraîche, along with the salty capers and smoked salmon, make the Belgian endive taste amazingly sweet. The same formula can be applied to other ingredients: for example, try mixing watercress with curly endive, sour orange juice and salty olives.

serves 6 as a starter

6 Belgian endive or red chicory, trimmed
2 small red onions, finely sliced
2 heaped tablespoons capers
200ml (7fl oz) crème fraîche
2 teaspoons lemon juice
2 tablespoons good extra virgin olive oil
salt and freshly ground black pepper
400g (14oz) 12 slices finely sliced smoked salmon
1½ lemons, cut into 12 wedges

1 Separate the Belgian endive leaves. Put in a large bowl with the finely sliced red onions. Rinse the capers and pat dry on kitchen paper. Whisk the crème fraîche in a small bowl with 2 tablespoons of cold water.

2 When you are ready to serve, drizzle the endive with the lemon juice and olive oil. Toss well, then lightly season with salt and freshly ground black pepper. Divide between 6 plates, then weave in the smoked salmon slices. Scatter with capers, then either lightly drizzle the crème fraîche over the salmon or serve it on the side. Put the lemon wedges on the plates. Serve immediately.

spicy scallop, curly endive and cucumber salad

This is a slight variation on the taste theme of the chicory, lemon and caper salad with smoked salmon on p.94. Here, sweet scallops, bitter-sweet cucumber and a sour vinaigrette work brilliantly with bitter curly endive. Salt is only added as a seasoning. The effect remains the same, in that the combination is incredibly moreish to eat.

serves 4

½ clove of garlic, finely chopped
2 dessertspoons white wine vinegar
6 dessertspoons extra virgin olive oil
salt and freshly ground black pepper
1 curly endive heart, trimmed
4 spring onions, trimmed and sliced
1 ridge cucumber, peeled
1 tablespoon sweet paprika
½ teaspoon each cayenne pepper, ground cumin and cinnamon
20 roeless, medium to small-sized cleaned scallops
2 tablespoons olive oil

1 Preheat an oven-top grill-pan over a medium heat. Whisk together the garlic, white wine vinegar and olive oil. Season to taste and set aside.

2 Place the leaves and spring onions in a big bowl. Slice the cucumber into half moons and add to the salad.

3 Mix together the paprika, cayenne pepper, cumin and cinnamon with a generous pinch of salt and some black pepper. Toss the scallops in the olive oil and coat in the mixed spice. Cook on the oven-top grill-pan for about 5 minutes, turning regularly. Meanwhile, dress the salad with the vinaigrette. Add the scallops and divide between 4 plates. Serve immediately.

watercress, pear and blue cheese salad

Another variation on the taste theme of the chicory salad on p.94. This time umami comes from the cheese, sweetness from the pears and a bitter-sourness from the walnut oil vinaigrette. Apples or peaches could replace the fruit, and salty feta cheese could be used instead of the gorgonzola.

serves 4

4 little gem lettuce hearts
55g (2oz) watercress, cut into sprigs
55g (2oz) walnut kernels
1 tablespoon white wine vinegar
3 tablespoons walnut oil
salt and freshly ground black pepper
2 small ripe pears
1 tablespoon lemon juice
170g (6oz) gorgonzola, cut into rough cubes

1 Separate the lettuce leaves and rip into big pieces. Wash and dry with the watercress sprigs, before placing in a large mixing bowl with walnut kernels. Whisk together the white wine vinegar and walnut oil, season to taste and set aside.

2 Peel, quarter and core the pears, tossing them in the lemon juice as you do so. Mix the pears into the salad with the blue cheese. Gently mix in the vinaigrette, adjust the seasoning to taste and serve on pretty plates with walnut bread.

grilled chicory with prosciutto and figs

When food is lightly brushed with lemon juice before being grilled, the juice cooks and adds a slight bitter-sour sweetness to the smoky grilled flavour. This enhances any sweetness in bitter ingredients, such as grilled Belgian endive, and in this recipe is echoed by the sweetness of the accompanying figs. The salty umami ham and bitter rocket enhance the taste of the endive further. Radicchio can be used instead of red chicory.

serves 6

3 sprigs of fresh lemon thyme
1½ tablespoons lemon juice
5 tablespoons extra virgin olive oil
salt and freshly ground black pepper
6 ripe figs
6 heads red chicory or Belgian endive
6 handfuls of wild rocket leaves
18 thin slices of prosciutto

1 Preheat an oven-top grill-pan over a low heat or use a barbecue when the coals have died down. Strip the thyme leaves from their stalks and place in a small mixing bowl with the lemon juice, olive oil and seasoning. Whisk together and pour half into a large mixing bowl. Trim the fig stems, cut each fig in half and set aside.

2 Trim off the base of each chicory and, depending on how fat they are, either halve or quarter lengthways. Gently wash under the cold tap, roughly shake off the excess water and toss in the large bowl with the vinaigrette. Place on the grill-pan or barbecue and grill for about 30 minutes, turning regularly and basting with the vinaigrette (from the large mixing bowl) as you do so. The chicory is cooked once it is soft and flecked golden brown.

3 Shortly before serving, dress the rocket with the remaining vinaigrette. Arrange in airy piles on 6 plates. Just before the chicory is ready, add the figs to the grill pan. As soon as they are soft and oozing with juice, remove with the chicory and arrange on the plates with the prosciutto. Serve immediately.

marinades

Bitterness is not widely used in marinades for two main reasons: first, unlike sour, salty or sweet ingredients in marinades, bitter ingredients do not affect the final texture of the food; and second, if too much bitterness is absorbed into a dish it will taste unpleasant. In other words, bitter ingredients such as orange zest or Angostura bitters tend to be added to marinades as a taste enhancer rather than as a dominant taste. Olive oil is a notable exception to this rule. Aside from being a useful carrier for other flavours, it is so mild that it imbues food with a suave bitter edge.

curried caribbean-style fish

Angostura bitters makes fish taste sweeter and fresher. Its taste is so subtle that the eater is only aware that the fish seems duller without it. This is particularly noticeable with prawns – try marinating them raw with garlic, adding a few drops of Angostura bitters to half of them, then compare the taste after grilling.

serves 6

8 spring onions, finely chopped
1 tablespoon finely chopped fresh lemon thyme
2 cloves of garlic, finely chopped
¼ teaspoon finely chopped habañero chilli, or to taste
2 limes, juiced
6 portions of gilt head bream or snapper fillet
½ teaspoon Angostura bitters
4 tablespoons sunflower oil
1 onion, finely sliced
1 tablespoon curry powder
400ml (14fl oz) canned coconut milk
salt and freshly ground black pepper

1 Mix the finely chopped spring onions, thyme, garlic and chilli with the lime juice. Remember that habañeros are very hot, so handle with caution. Trim the fish fillets, removing any bones, then rub with Angostura bitters before coating in the marinade. Leave, covered and chilled, to marinate for 20–30 minutes.

2 Set a wide, shallow saucepan over a low heat. Once hot, add the oil and onion and gently fry for 10 minutes, until soft and golden. Stir in the curry powder and cook for a further 4 minutes.

3 Increase the heat and push the onion to one side in the pan. Add some of the marinated fish, flesh-side-down. Fry briskly until lightly coloured, then flip over and cook for another minute. Remove the half-cooked fish and set aside. Repeat the process until all the fish is seared. Add the remaining lime marinade and the coconut milk, reduce the heat and bring to the boil. Simmer gently for 10 minutes, then return the fish fillets to the pan and poach for 5 minutes. This is scrumptious eaten with steamed rice and spinach.

crispy fried beef with chilli and orange

Dried bitter orange zest is far more intense than fresh. It adds as much fragrance as taste to this dish. Note also that the sauce is another salty-sweet-sour variation – perfect for enhancing the delicate bitter note that the orange zest introduces to the meat and making it a delectable dish.

serves 4

2 strips of finely pared bitter orange peel
2 teaspoons Szechuan peppercorns
1 teaspoon cornflour
salt
340g (12oz) lean beef, such as rump or topside
2⅔ tablespoons sunflower oil, plus extra for deep-frying
2 large carrots, peeled
6 tablespoons caster sugar
4½ tablespoons rice or wine vinegar
3 tablespoons good soy sauce
1 tablespoon finely shredded fresh ginger
2 cloves of garlic, finely shredded
1 teaspoon dried chilli flakes
1 red pepper, quartered, seeded and finely sliced
4 spring onions, finely sliced

1 Put the orange peel into the oven and turn it to 150°C (300°F) gas mark 2. Bake for about 30 minutes, until dry and fragrant. Meanwhile, put the Szechuan peppercorns in a small dry-frying pan over a medium heat. As soon as they smell fragrant, remove and put in a spice grinder or pestle and mortar. Add the dried orange peel. Grind both to a powder and mix with the cornflour and a pinch of salt. Cut the beef into long thin matchsticks, mix into the cornflour and marinate for 20 minutes. Then, using your hands, mix in 2 teaspoons of sunflower oil until all the beef strands are separate.

2 Cut the carrots into fine sticks roughly the same size as the beef. Heat the oil in a deep fat fryer to 200°C (400°F). Carefully add some of the beef – the fat will froth up – and cook for 30 seconds, until firm. Remove and drain on kitchen paper. Once the oil returns to 200°C (400°F) repeat the process until all the beef is cooked. Lower the temperature to 190°C (375°F) and add the carrots in batches. Deep-fry for 2 minutes, or until they are golden with a slightly dry, almost crisp texture. Remove and drain on kitchen paper, then add to the beef.

3 Mix together the sugar, vinegar and soy sauce and set aside. When ready, heat 2 tablespoons of oil in a non-stick frying pan or wok. Add the ginger, stir-fry for a few seconds, then add the garlic, chilli flakes and sliced red pepper. Cook for 30 seconds, then add the sugar, vinegar and soy sauce mixture. Once hot, mix in the beef, deep-fried carrots and spring onions. Heat through and serve immediately with steamed rice.

sauces

Sauces are a useful means of adding bitterness to a dish, since the eater can control how much is added to their food. Normally, diners are unaware it is the bitter element in a sauce that makes a dish taste so interesting. Mayonnaise, for example, is not often thought of as a bitter sauce, despite the fact that chefs often lessen its bitterness by diluting the olive oil with a tasteless sunflower oil.

Bitter sauces enhance the natural sweetness of their accompaniment by making it less cloying and more complex in taste. These sauces can be divided into four main types: bitter-salt (tapenade); bitter-sweet (chocolate or coffee sauce); bitter-salt-sour (mayonnaise or vinaigrette); and bitter-sweet-sour (cranberry or Cumberland sauce). The skill of the cook lies in choosing the best combination to enhance a dish. The sweet sour nature of a bitter cranberry sauce, for example, will make bland roast turkey taste fresh and sweet, while its bitter component will add a depth of taste and interest that is impossible to achieve with a purely sweet-sour sauce like redcurrant jelly. Similarly, a bitter-sweet pudding sauce, such as chocolate, will enhance the subtle sweet dairy tastes of pancakes, ice-cream *et al*, in a satisfying manner.

grilled chicken with tomato, basil and olive sauce

The olive oil adds a delicate bitterness to this dish that is reinforced by the olives and lemon zest. There are myriad variations – the olives can be replaced by grilled, slightly bitter courgettes, fresh herbs or sweet roasted pepper. This sauce is wonderful with any grilled meat or fish.

serves 4

12 tablespoons good, peppery extra virgin olive oil
zest of 1 lemon, finely grated
2 small cloves of garlic, finely diced
2 tablespoons finely sliced basil leaves
4 boneless chicken breasts, skinned
salt and freshly ground black pepper
4 medium tomatoes, peeled and quartered
10 large green olives, stoned
1 teaspoon lemon juice

1 Make the marinade by mixing together 4 tablespoons of olive oil with the lemon zest, half the garlic and half the basil. Put the rest of the garlic and basil in a separate bowl with 8 tablespoons of olive oil for the sauce.

2 Trim the chicken breasts of any fat and remove their fillets. Place each breast between 2 sheets of clingfilm and gently beat with a rolling pin until they form 4 thin escalopes. Mix into the marinade with the fillets and season with black pepper. Cover and chill until needed.

3 Place a strainer over the bowl of basil oil. Cut away the tomato seeds, dropping them into the sieve. Strain the tomato juice into the bowl, sieving out the seeds. Cut the tomato flesh and olives into strips, and add to the bowl. Season with lemon juice, salt and pepper. If the tomatoes are very acidic you may not need lemon juice. Preheat an oven-top grill-pan over a medium-high heat. Once hot, cook the chicken for 4 minutes on each side. Serve with the sauce spooned over each breast.

roast duck with port and bitter orange sauce

Here is a bitter-sweet-sour-umami sauce. The sauce is made from a reduced umami duck stock, and finished with sweet-sour port and bitter orange zest. The bitterness of the orange zest mitigates any slight bloody bitterness of the duck (wild duck in particular has a tendency towards bitterness). This is a long recipe but it is easy to make. The resulting duck is crisp and succulent.

serves 8

2 oven-ready ducks, about 1.4kg (3lb) weight
2 teaspoons fine sea salt

stock

2 cloves of garlic
2 large carrots, peeled and roughly chopped
½ celeriac, peeled and roughly chopped
1 large onion, peeled and roughly chopped
½ bottle good red wine
a few sprigs each of fresh thyme and parsley
1 bay leaf
3 black peppercorns

sauce

peel of 1 Seville orange, finely pared
115ml (4fl oz) Port

1 Preheat the oven to its highest setting. Prick the ducks all over with a fork and rub the salt into their skin. Arrange upside-down in the roasting pan and roast for 10 minutes, then turn breast-side-up and roast for another 10 minutes. Remove and cool. Once cold, carve each bird into 8 pieces by removing the whole legs, which are then each cut in half through their joint and neatly trimmed. Then cut the breast meat away from the rib cage and cut each breast into 2 equal-sized pieces. Trim, cover and chill the portions.

2 Roughly chop the duck carcasses (removing the parsons' noses) and return to the roasting pan. Roast for 15 minutes, then mix in the garlic and vegetables and return to the oven for 15 minutes. Stir occasionally until flecked golden brown. Pour off any fat and transfer the bones and vegetables to a saucepan. Add the wine, herbs and peppercorns. Cover generously with water. Bring to the boil, skim, then simmer gently for 3 hours, or until it tastes good. Strain, cool and chill.

3 Dry the orange peel in the oven (on its lowest setting) for an hour. Skim off any fat from the stock and pour all but the cloudy bottom dregs into a clean saucepan. Boil vigorously until it is reduced by about three-quarters and tastes delicious. It can be frozen at this stage. You will need 600ml (1 generous pint) of reduced stock for the sauce. Add the dried orange peel and Port and boil for about 5 minutes, or until it has reduced to a syrupy consistency. Leave to infuse while you cook the duck. Return to the boil, strain and serve.

4 Preheat the grill to medium-high. Once hot, place the duck pieces, skin-side up, under the grill for 5 minutes, then turn and grill for another 5 minutes (large ducks may need a further 5 minutes). Serve hot with the sauce.

savoury dishes

Creating a savoury dish that both satisfies and stimulates the taste buds is never easy. Bitter ingredients in particular need careful handling if they are to dominate a recipe. First, you have to decide whether to modify their bitterness in the cooking method. Second, you must consider their texture. Some people have a marked dislike for bitter food if it becomes overly soft – think of mushy aubergines or a wet curry of slippery bitter Indian gourds – so it is important to consider how to create an appetizing texture. A crisp fried Parmesan-coated aubergine slice (see page 69), for example, will woo any aubergine hater, just as a dry curry of gourds makes them succulent. Lastly, you must consider which tastes will work well with the intrinsic bitterness of the main ingredient. Salty-umami foods such as cheese, soy sauce or ham, make bitterness taste sweeter and less bitter, as do sweet ingredients such as cream, eggs or honey. Sour seasonings introduce a freshness, lightening the overall taste, as do other bitter ingredients, if used lightly.

chicory gratin with bacon

Bitter ingredients such as chicory will always taste sweeter if combined with salty ingredients such as bacon or Taleggio cheese. Here, the chicory has been initially gently grilled to reduce its natural bitterness – this also imbues it with an intriguing smoky flavour. Other brassicas such as cauliflower might be blanched instead of grilled before following the same method.

serves 2

3 fat Belgian endives, quartered lengthways
½ small lemon, juiced
4 tablespoons olive oil
salt and freshly ground black pepper
a generous pinch of chilli powder
225g (8oz) smoked back bacon, diced
170g (6oz) Taleggio cheese

1 Preheat an oven-top grill-pan over a medium-low heat and preheat the oven to 200°C (400°F) gas mark 6.

2 Gently wash the endive quarters under the cold tap. Roughly shake off the excess water and place in a large mixing bowl. Toss in the lemon juice with a tablespoon of olive oil. Gently rub in salt, freshly ground black pepper and chilli powder to taste, then arrange on the grill-pan. Turn regularly, brushing with a further tablespoon of olive oil if necessary. They will take about 30 minutes, depending on their size. They are cooked once soft and flecked golden brown.

3 Meanwhile, fry the bacon in 2 tablespoons olive oil until crisp. Spoon half over the base of a small ovenproof baking dish. Cover with the cooked endives, arranged in a single layer, and scatter with the remaining bacon. Cut the rind off the Taleggio cheese, slice, and roughly cover the endives. Place in the oven and bake for 15 minutes until bubbling, hot and flecked gold. Try serving with a tomato salad and crusty bread.

stir-fried spring greens with mustard seeds

Here, bitter mustard seeds complement the bitter leaves, while soy sauce adds a touch of umami and salt.

serves 2

200g (7oz) spring greens
3 thinly sliced rounds of fresh ginger
2 tablespoons sunflower oil
1 clove of garlic, finely sliced
1 teaspoon white mustard seeds
1 tablespoon soy sauce

1 Wash the greens, then strip away and discard any tough or damaged outer leaves along with the stems. Break up the hearts, ripping up any larger leaves. Set aside.

2 Fry the ginger in oil over a medium-high heat. Once it starts to sizzle and turn golden, add the garlic and mustard seeds. Stir-fry for 3 seconds, then increase the heat and mix in the spring greens. Stir-fry briskly until they wilt, then mix in the soy sauce. Discard the ginger and serve.

olive oil and sea salt bread

Many inherently sweet ingredients such as potatoes and flour benefit from the mild bitterness of good olive oil.

makes 1 loaf (serves 6)

450g (1lb) Italian '00' flour
1 teaspoon fine sea salt
1½ teaspoons easy-blend dried yeast
5½ tablespoons extra virgin olive oil
55g (2oz) pitted green olives, cut into chunks
1 teaspoon coarse sea salt

1 Put the flour and salt in a big bowl. Mix in the yeast, then add 340ml (12fl oz) tepid water until you have a soft dough. Turn out on to a floured surface and knead until smooth, then flatten and indent. Add 2 tablespoons of olive oil. Gently fold over and knead into the dough. Repeat with 2 more tablespoons of oil. Add the olives and knead for 5 minutes, or until smooth and supple. Add a tablespoon of olive oil to a large bowl and tip in the soft dough, lightly coating it in the oil. Cover the bowl with clingfilm and leave in a warm place for 2 hours, or until the dough has doubled in size. Keep out of draughts.

2 Turn out the dough and knock back. Shape into a circle on a heavy baking sheet. Loosely cover with a clean cloth and leave to rise for an hour, or until soft and spongy. Preheat the oven to its highest setting. Mix ½ tablespoon of olive oil with ¼ teaspoon of water. Make large soft indentations in the dough with your fingers, then brush with oil and water. Sprinkle with sea salt, then bake for 12-15 minutes, or until the bread is golden and sounds hollow when tapped. Eat while warm.

watercress crème fraîche tart

The bitterness of the watercress is lightened by the addition of the mildly acidic crème fraîche in this tart. Salt is also added in the form of bacon. Variations might include smoked salmon in place of the bacon or sour cream instead of crème fraîche.

serves 4

225g (8oz) shortcrust pastry (see page 203)
200g (7oz) back bacon
3 tablespoons olive oil
2 medium onions, finely diced
85g (3oz) watercress
1 whole egg
1 egg yolk
200ml (7fl oz) crème fraîche
5g (¼oz) Parmesan cheese, finely grated
salt and freshly ground black pepper

1 Preheat the oven to 200°C (400°F) gas mark 6. Roll out the pastry on a lightly floured surface into a 30cm (12-inch) circle and loosely wrap around the rolling pin. Hold the pin over a 23cm (9-inch) tart dish and carefully unroll, gently pressing the pastry into place. Prick the bottom with a fork, press some greaseproof paper into the middle, and fill with baking beans before chilling for 30 minutes.

2 Place the tart in the centre of the preheated oven and bake blind for 15 minutes. Remove the weighted paper and continue to bake for another 2 minutes, or until the pastry has become dry but not coloured and has lost that raw, sweaty look.

3 While the pastry is cooking, remove the fat from the bacon and dice. Heat the oil in a large frying pan and briskly fry the bacon for 2 minutes. Stir in the diced onions, reduce the heat and fry for 8 minutes, or until soft and golden. Tip the mixture into a bowl.

4 Wash the watercress and strip it of its leaves, discarding the stalks and any yellow or slimy leaves. Place in a food processor with the egg and egg yolk. Process until the watercress leaves are finely chopped (this can be done by hand if necessary). Mix in the crème fraîche, then stir into the sautéed bacon with the Parmesan. Adjust the seasoning to taste and pour into the tart case. Place in the oven, reduce the temperature to 180°C (350°F) gas mark 4, and bake for 40 minutes, or until the filling is just set and golden brown. Serve hot, warm or cold.

sautéed veal escalopes with watercress

A simple cream sauce is transformed by the addition of watercress, giving it a mildly bitter edge. This is further enlivened by the bitter vermouth and sour lemon juice. The same result would be achieved with finely sliced spinach, since that too has an element of bitterness in its leaves. In either case, it enhances the sweetness of sautéed fish or other meat such as chicken, turkey or pork escalopes.

serves 4

285g (10oz) watercress
4 veal escalopes
salt and freshly ground black pepper
3 tablespoons olive oil
1 fat shallot, halved and finely sliced
4 tablespoons extra dry vermouth
285ml (½ pint) double cream
2 teaspoons lemon juice

1 Place a serving plate in the oven and preheat to its lowest setting. Wash the watercress and strip of its leaves, taking care to discard any that are yellow or slimy. Set these aside.

2 Trim the escalopes of any thin membrane and, if not suitably thin, place between 2 sheets of clingfilm and gently but firmly beat with a rolling pin or meat hammer. Season with salt and ground black pepper.

3 Set a large non-stick frying pan over a medium high heat. Once hot, add a tablespoon of olive oil and briskly fry half the veal escalopes for 1–2 minutes on each side. Transfer to the warm serving plate, add another tablespoon of oil, and repeat the process with the remaining escalopes.

4 Allow the frying pan to cool, then set over a low heat and, if necessary, add a tablespoon of oil. Gently fry the shallot for a couple of minutes until soft, then pour in the vermouth, boil until it has reduced by half. Immediately add the cream with 4 tablespoons water and the watercress and simmer gently for 5 minutes or until the watercress has collapsed into a soft creamy mess. Return the veal escalopes to the pan, stirring their juices into the sauce. Simmer for 3 minutes and then mix in the lemon juice and season to taste. Serve immediately with a saffron-infused chicken stock pilaff (see p.200).

puddings and cakes

The aim of a pudding or cake is to 'close the stomach'. In other words, hunger and the gustatory desire for exciting tastes is satiated. The best way to achieve this is to serve a bitter-sweet pudding, since it is both exciting and satisfying to eat. If, however, you add sourness to the mixture you may find that your guests still crave a dark chocolate to finish their meal. Imagine eating a lemon gin and tonic jelly, for example, and compare how you might feel after a mocha mousse.

Many bitter-sweet puddings taste particularly good if you combine two bitter ingredients – coffee and chocolate, chocolate and bitter orange, caramel and coffee, or bitter almond essence with chocolate, for example. All bitter-sweet puddings and cakes, however, are dependent on being diluted, regardless of whether it is with water, cream, butter or eggs. Some bitter ingredients, such as Angostura bitters, almond essence and citrus zest, can only be used in small quantities.

bitter orange syllabub

An amazingly rich but delicious syllabub, in which orange zest and brandy add a bitter edge to a sweet-sour dish. The same principles apply to other syllabubs and bitter-sweet fruit fools such as cranberry or plum. This recipe can be made in advance, but you will need to rewhisk it as the alcohol separates slightly from the cream.

serves 6

2 Seville oranges
3 tablespoons good brandy, such as Rémy-Martin
55g (2oz) caster sugar
85ml (3fl oz) good white dessert wine
565ml (1 pint) chilled double cream

1 Finely pare the rind from 1 Seville orange, making sure that none of the white pith is attached. Place the peel in a small mixing bowl with the brandy and sugar. Cover and leave for a minimum of 12 hours, or until needed. The zest will imbue the brandy with a superb orange flavour.

2 Shortly before serving, remove the sugary peel from the brandy and cut it into neat fine strips. Set aside. Scrape the sugary liquid into a large mixing bowl. Then, using a zester, finely grate the rind from the remaining orange and mix into the brandy with the dessert wine and the juice from 1½ Seville oranges.

3 Shortly before serving, pour the brandy into the double cream and whisk until it forms soft peaks; this will happen very quickly. Spoon into pretty glasses and decorate with the julienned brandied peel. Serve within 30 minutes.

coffee crème caramel

A sexy bitter-sweet pudding, in which a bitter-sweet coffee custard is given greater resonance by its caramel sauce. Custard can be imbued with many different bitter tastes, such as bitter orange zest or chocolate.

serves 6

425ml (¾ pint) milk
140ml (¼ pint) single cream
4 tablespoons medium ground coffee
55g (2oz) caster sugar
2 medium eggs
2 medium egg yolks
a pinch of freshly grated nutmeg

caramel
115g (4oz) granulated sugar

1 Preheat an oven to 160°C (310°F) gas mark 2½. Put the milk, cream, ground coffee and caster sugar into a saucepan. Set over a medium heat and bring to the boil, then remove from the heat, stir once and leave to infuse for 30 minutes.

2 Cut 6 greaseproof paper discs to fit the top of 6 x 140ml (¼ pint) soufflé dishes. To make the caramel, put the granulated sugar and 4 tablespoons of water in a small heavy bottomed saucepan. Dissolve the sugar over a low heat, then increase the heat and boil rapidly without stirring until it turns a beautiful golden caramel. Immediately remove from the heat and pour into each dish, swirling as you do so to ensure that each base is well coated in the caramel. Place the soufflé dishes in a roasting tray.

3 Put the whole eggs and egg yolks in a large bowl. Gently whisk together with a fork (try not to over-whisk or the caramel will be full of air-bubbles). Strain in the coffee milk mixture through a fine sieve and gently stir into the eggs. Season with nutmeg and strain through a coarse sieve into a pouring jug. Divide between the 6 dishes.

4 Wet and scrumple the greaseproof paper discs before placing on top of each custard. Pour enough water into the roasting tray to come half-way up the soufflé dishes and transfer to the oven. Reduce the heat to 150°C (300°F) gas mark 2 and bake for 23 minutes, or until just set. Allow to cool, then chill until needed. When ready to serve, remove the paper discs, very gently loosen the top of each custard, and invert it on to an individual serving bowl. The caramel sauce will spill out around the coffee custard.

chocolate profiteroles

Bitter sweet sauces are widely used with creamy, sweet puddings to add that final, satisfying contrast of taste. The delicate sweet-salty nature of a cream-filled choux bun, for example, is a perfect medium to experiment with a bitter-sweet sauce, regardless of whether it is based on chocolate, coffee or caramel. However, such sauces should be used with care when accompanying sweet-sour puddings.

serves 6

choux pastry

sunflower oil for greasing
115g (4oz) plain flour
a pinch of salt
115g (4oz) butter, diced
4 small eggs, roughly beaten

chocolate sauce

170g (6oz) dark chocolate
115g (4oz) caster sugar

filling

3 tablespoons kirsch
285ml (½ pint) double cream

1 Begin by making the choux pastry. Preheat the oven to 200°C (400°F) gas mark 6. Oil 2 non-stick baking trays. Sift the flour and salt and set aside. Pour 300ml (scant 11fl oz) water into a small saucepan and add the diced butter. Bring to a brisk boil and, as soon as the butter has melted, take off the heat and tip in the flour. Return to a low heat and, using a wooden spoon, beat vigorously for 3–4 minutes until the mixture is smooth and glossy and leaves the side of the saucepan. Remove from the heat and continue to beat for 1–2 minutes before slowly beating in the eggs, a little at a time. Make sure each bit of egg is absorbed into the dough before adding the next. Stop when the dough is smooth and glossy but stiff enough to hold its shape.

2 Using a pudding spoon, drop 24 walnut-sized choux pastry blobs on to the baking sheets, making sure that there is plenty of space between the profiteroles. Bake for 15 minutes, or until dry and crisp, then quickly pierce each one and return them to the switched-off oven for a further 5 minutes, with the door open. This allows any steam to escape. Transfer to a cooling rack and leave until cold.

3 For the chocolate sauce, break up the chocolate into small pieces and place in a small saucepan with 285ml (½ pint) water. Melt over a low heat, stirring occasionally, until smooth. Add the sugar and stir until dissolved, then simmer for 20 minutes, stirring occasionally, until it forms a rich sauce.

4 Pour the kirsch and cream into a large mixing bowl. Whisk until the cream forms soft peaks. Pipe into the profiteroles and arrange in an artistic pile. When ready to serve, reheat the sauce and pour over the profiteroles.

hazelnut mocha roulade

Bitter-sweet tastes play with one another here, as roasted and therefore mildly bitter hazelnuts are made into a sweet sponge that is then filled with a bitter-sweet coffee chocolate butter. There are all sorts of bitter sweet sponge variations, including coffee walnut cake and chocolate almond cake.

serves 6-8

sunflower oil for greasing
115g (4oz) shelled hazelnuts
2 level tablespoons plain flour
a pinch of salt
½ teaspoon baking powder
6 medium eggs, separated
115g (4oz) caster sugar

mocha butter cream

55g (2oz) dark chocolate
2 teaspoons instant coffee
115g (4oz) softened unsalted butter
115g (4oz) icing sugar, sifted

1 Preheat the oven to 180°C (350°F) gas mark 4. Line a 35cm (14 inch) x 25cm (10 inch) shallow baking tray with greaseproof paper, carefully cutting at each corner so that it stands up above the tray. Secure with paper clips and lightly oil.

2 Place the hazelnuts on a second tray and roast for 10 minutes, until they release a glorious scent. Remove and tip into a clean tea-towel. Rub vigorously to remove their papery brown skins. Place the clean nuts in a food processor. Once cool, process in short bursts until they are finely ground. Add the flour, salt and baking powder and whiz once more to mix thoroughly.

3 Put the egg yolks and all but 2 tablespoons of the caster sugar in a larger bowl and whisk until they from a pale mousse that holds a trail. Then whisk the egg whites until they form floppy peaks. Add 2 tablespoons of caster sugar and whisk for a further minute, or until glossy. Using a metal spoon, quickly fold the hazelnut mixture into the egg yolks, followed by the whites. Pour into the lined baking tray and bake for 8 minutes or until just cooked and shrinking away from the tray rim.

4 Once the roulade is cool enough to handle, turn it out on to a sheet of greaseproof paper. Cover with a cloth and leave until cold.

5 Meanwhile, break up the chocolate and place in a small bowl. Dissolve the coffee with 2-3 teaspoons boiling water and add to the chocolate. Set over a bowl of just boiled water and stir occasionally until it has melted. Remove from the heat and leave to cool until tepid while you beat together the butter and icing sugar until fluffy, then mix in the cool melted coffee chocolate. Spread over the cold roulade then, using the paper, tightly roll up the roulade so it forms a long Swiss roll. Trim the edges and ease on to a serving dish. Chill.

catherine's chocolate cake

Unfortunately, the lightness of this recipe slightly belies my premise that one is satisfied with a bitter-sweet dish. It is easy to eat this cake in a day, despite the fact that it improves if left for 24 hours. Catherine, incidentally, was a French *au pair* who briefly looked after my brother and me when we were very small, and is still remembered for this heavenly cake.

serves 6

55g (2oz) butter, diced, plus extra for buttering
20g (¾oz) plain flour, plus extra for dusting
115g (4oz) dark chocolate
3 medium eggs, separated
85g (3oz) caster sugar
a pinch of salt
a few drops vanilla essence

1 Preheat the oven to 180°C (350°F) gas mark 4. Butter a 20cm (8 inch) spring-form cake tin, then lightly dust it with flour. Set aside.

2 Break the chocolate into small pieces and put in a bowl that will neatly fit over a pan of just boiled water (off the heat). You may need to replace the water half-way through the melting time. Once the chocolate is nearly melted, add the butter and stir until it has melted. Remove from the hot water.

3 Whisk the egg yolks with the sugar and mix in a pinch of salt, then fold in the tepid chocolate butter mixture and vanilla essence with a metal spoon. Immediately sift the flour over the chocolate mixture and fold it in. Quickly whisk the egg whites until they form soft peaks, and then fold them into the chocolate mixture.

4 Pour the mixture into the prepared cake tin and bake in the centre of the oven for about 25 minutes. The cake will puff up and form a slight crust as it cooks. It should be almost cooked after 25 minutes – test by inserting a skewer into the centre of the cake; if it comes out almost clean, the cake is ready. Remove from the oven. Once it is cool enough to handle, gently turn out on to a cooling rack (it is very fragile). Once cold it should be moist yet light.

caramelized banana tartlets

Angostura bitters works in conjunction with bitter-sweet caramelized sugar and sour lime juice to make the banana tartlets taste utterly gorgeous. One is never enough!

makes 6

pastry

115g (4oz) plain flour
a pinch of salt
55g (2oz) softened, roughly diced butter
55g (2oz) caster sugar
2 egg yolks

topping

4 small bananas
1 lime, juiced
½ teaspoon Angostura bitters
1-2 tablespoons demerara sugar

1 To make the pastry, sift the flour and salt on to a clean work surface. Make a small well in the centre and place the other ingredients in the middle. Using the fingertips of one hand, lightly jab the butter, sugar and egg yolks until they are worked together. Then, using a palette knife, flip and cut the flour into this soft mixture until it forms chunks of soft dough. Lightly knead the mixture into a smooth dough. Wrap in a polythene bag and chill for 2 hours.

2 Preheat the oven to 190°C (375°F) gas mark 5. Roll out the pastry and stamp out 8 rounds, each 7.5cm (3-inches) in diameter. Slip on to a heavy non-stick baking sheet and prick each biscuit with a fork. Chill for 30 minutes, then bake for about 5-6 minutes, or until a very pale biscuit colour.

3 Meanwhile, cut the bananas into medium-thick rounds. Toss in the lime juice and Angostura bitters and arrange in a concentric circle over the pastry bases. Sprinkle with brown sugar and return to the oven for 8-10 minutes, or until the bananas are cooked. Remove and gently slip on to a cooling rack. The pastry is still soft at this stage; it will become firmer as it cools. Serve warm or tepid with crème fraîche or sour cream.

preserves

Bitter-tasting foods make good preserves, as their bitterness acts as a strong and vivid-tasting counterbalance to the large quantities of sugar, vinegar and/or salt needed when preserving. The most obvious example is Seville oranges, as their bitter pith and peel is transformed into a luscious delicacy with sugar, regardless of whether they are made into marmalade or succade (candied peel in syrup).

The same is true of many wild bitter-sour fruits, such as rowanberries, sloes and crab apples, all of which make excellent pickles and jellies. Bitter gherkins, cauliflower, cabbage and such like all taste sweeter for salting before being preserved in vinegar. The addition of bitter flavourings, such as mustard seeds can also enhance the sweetness of a primary bitter ingredient.

bitter marmalade

A mere tablespoon of equally bitter black treacle will deepen and enhance the natural bitterness of Seville oranges in this ultra-orangey marmalade.

makes 2.3kg (5lb)

900g (2lb) Seville oranges
2 lemons
1.4kg (3lb) granulated sugar
1 tablespoon black treacle

1 Wash the fruit and place in a big pan with 1.7 litres (3 pints) water. Cover tightly, bring to the boil and simmer gently for 1½ hours, until the fruit is soft and easily pierced. Transfer the fruit to a bowl, leaving the cooking liquid in its pan. Once the fruit is cool enough to handle, slice it in half and, with a spoon, scrape out the pulp, pips and most of the pith into a bowl. Return these to the pan with the cooking liquid, making sure the pulp is thoroughly mashed up. Bring back to the boil and reduce by half, then strain it into a jam pan.

2 Preheat the oven to 140°C (275°F) gas mark 1. To sterilize your jam jars, wash in soapy water, rinse and put them in a preheated oven for 10 minutes, or until dry.

3 Meanwhile, finely slice the fruit skins into thin strips and add to the jam pan. Clip on the thermometer, return to the boil, then mix in the sugar and treacle. Stir until the sugar has dissolved, then bring to the boil and allow to reach jam setting point – 105°C (221°F) – which should take about 10 minutes once the sugar has melted. Skim, then leave to settle for about 15 minutes, stirring occasionally. Pour into the warm dry sterilized jam jars and cover with paper discs. Seal and label once cold.

bitter notes

Caramelized sugar is a useful way of adding a little sweet bitterness to a wide variety of dishes. Demerara or white sugar can be sprinkled on to fruit, such as kumquats, figs, apples or peaches, and then caramelized under the grill. Cakes and whipped cream puddings can be drizzled in caramelized sugar, while crème brulées can be sprinkled with sugar and finished under the grill.

Bitter-sweet-sour fruit jellies, such as damson, rowanberry, crab apple, elderberry or cranberry, add an instant bitter note to a meal. This is particularly useful if serving roast game such as pheasant or wild duck, as the taste counteracts any underlying 'bloody' bitterness in the meat. A spoonful or two can also be added to fruit pies if a deeper, more rounded taste is needed. Try elderberry or damson jelly with plum or blackberry puddings, or rowanberry or crab apple jelly with apple puddings.

A dusting of cocoa adds a delicate bitter bite to a pudding, cake or truffle. Cocoa's intense bitter chocolate taste resonates with sweet recipes that have a bitter element, such as nut cakes, creamy coffee puddings or rich chocolate dishes. Aside from chocolate truffles, sift cocoa over the dish at the last minute and avoid getting it on your clothes – it's murder to remove.

The bitter-sweet nature of mayonnaise emphasizes the sweetness of foods such as raw vegetables, boiled eggs, chicken, salmon and shellfish. It is easy to make in a small food processor. Mix 2 egg yolks with salt, freshly ground pepper, ½ tablespoon tarragon vinegar (or lemon juice) and a teaspoon of Dijon mustard. Whizz until pale and frothy, then slowly add 285ml (½ pint) olive oil, initially drop by drop and then, as it thickens, in a thin stream. If it gets too thick, add more vinegar. Adjust the seasonings to taste.

Occasionally, bitter garnishes can be put to good use. Deep-fried parsley or basil leaves, for example, will add a crisp, bitter note to everything from salads to grilled fish or meat. Use the freshest herb leaves and make sure that they are completely dry before dropping them into some sunflower oil at 150°C (300°F) for just a few seconds, or until they are dark and translucent in appearance and crisp in texture.

Lemon, lime or orange zest will give a hint of bitterness to a wide variety of dishes. It can be finely grated and added to marinades for fish or meat, or beaten into cakes, puddings and creams. Finely pared citrus zest can be infused into sugar-syrups for fruit salads and custards and, when it is julienned (cut into very fine strips), it can be blanched and then simmered in syrup to garnish puddings and cakes.

Olives are naturally bitter as well as salty. They are therefore a useful addition to salads and sauces. Tapenade is perhaps the most intense example of the latter, and consequently should be used cautiously so as not to dominate other foods. De-salt 8 anchovy fillets by soaking in milk for 20 minutes, then rinse, dry and process with 24 stoned black olives, 2 tablespoons of rinsed and dried capers, 3 tablespoons of canned tuna, a hint of garlic and a few drops of brandy. Once smooth, dilute and season to taste with lemon juice and olive oil. The mixture should form a thick paste.

Freshly grated peeled horseradish will introduce a bitter taste if whisked into a vinaigrette or cream sauce. The former is delicious with sweet beetroot, green beans and little gem lettuce hearts, while the latter is excellent with smoked fish, cooked salmon or beef.

sweet

Sweetness is synonymous with pleasure. The intense physical delight experienced when we eat a spoonful of honey or some sugary cake is rooted in our need to ingest carbohydrates. In the same way that our repugnance of very bitter or sour tastes protects us from eating poisonous or spoilt food, so the pleasure we find in sweet-tasting ingredients encourages us to devour necessary carbohydrates, regardless of whether this is in the form of a ripe fig or a sweet ear of wheat.

A sound understanding of sweetness will allow any cook to conjure up delectable dishes. A curl of sweet butter on new potatoes, for example, is just as taste-enhancing as a sprinkling of sugar on strawberries. We are all born with different perceptions of sweetness, but the more sweet food we consume, the less sweetness we can taste. Nor is our sensitivity restricted to common sugars such as sucrose, glucose and fructose; chemically unrelated sweet tastes such as chloroform, and artificial sweeteners such as aspartame and saccharin, also taste sweet. Incidentally, it is worth noting that many ready-made savoury foods contain some form of sweetening to make them, in theory at least, more appetizing. The gastronomically brave should try (temporarily) cutting out excess sugar from their diet to see how it affects their perception of taste. After the initial torture of sourness, you will find that amazingly delicate nuances of taste appear in everything from sweet carrots to tart apples.

Sweetness can be found in grains, fruits, vegetables, animal fat, shellfish, milk and nuts. Once recognized, it is an easy matter to apply the other tastes to enhance this element in your food. A pinch of salt, for example, intensifies sweetness, making a dish taste satisfying rather than stimulating; try toast spread with salty butter and honey. Umami also heightens sweetness, but in an exciting way. Thus prawns taste wonderfully sweet stir-fried with soy sauce. A liberal dash of sourness lessens sweetness, while a little sourness can have the opposite effect, but in either instance the food will taste lighter and more refreshing. Swirl tart crème fraîche into a naturally sweet pea soup and you will want a second helping. A moderate amount of bitterness will also reduce sweetness, but in an intriguing way that teases and satiates the appetite, often tempting the cook to add a little refreshing sourness. Sautéed sugared bananas, for example, are good with a dash of Angostura bitters, but better with lime juice too.

Like all tastes, sweetness needs to be handled sensitively; there is danger of over-enhancing it in recipes, which would result in sickly, bland food. It has to be diluted when too strong and enhanced when too weak. You can even use one form of sweetness to enhance another. A pancake, for example, is naturally sweet with its milk, eggs and flour, but drizzle it with maple syrup and you will taste luscious new depths. Ultimately, sweetness should be used to create exciting, appetizing, yet satisfying food.

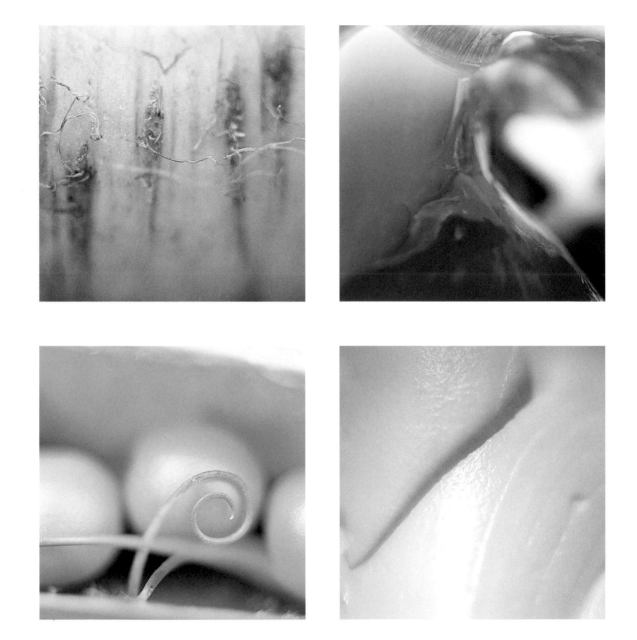

parsnips

Parsnips *(Pastinaca sativa)*, like carrots and beetroot, contain a high level of sugar (around 6%) in their plump, cream-coloured roots. They also contain the same amount of starch, which some say will turn to sugar if the unfortunate parsnip is exposed to the first frost of the winter. Their inherent sweetness makes them a useful source of sweetness in savoury dishes, despite the fact that for centuries British cooks preferred to feed them to their pigs.

Parsnips' sweetness can be intensified by frying or roasting. A by-product of this method is that their sugar caramelizes on the outside, imbuing them with a satisfying hint of bitterness, especially if seasoned with a little salt. Alternatively, their sweetness can be tempered by sour ingredients, such as with a tart vinaigrette, or increased by umami, for example with a good beef or duck gravy.

peas

Garden peas *(Pisum sativium)* have two dominant tastes: sweetness and umami (peas contain about 200mg per 100g of free glutamate), which accounts for their intriguing, savoury-sweet lure. Given these dual tastes, peas need salt to counterbalance their intense sweetness by emphasizing their savoury umami nature. Yet salt also accentuates peas' sweetness, an effect that can be lessened by adding soured cream or bitter-tasting lettuce, cucumber or rocket. Combine peas with umami-tasting ingredients such as Parmesan, stock or shellfish and their sweetness is increased.

As soon as a pea is picked it starts to convert its sugar into starch, just as it does if left to mature on the plant – hence the mealy nature of fat, old peas. Prompt chilling of freshly picked peas slows down this conversion.

scallops

Scallops have a sweet, natural taste that the Chinese describe as '*hsien*'. Unlike the intense umami taste of a reduced stock, '*hsien*' has an artlessness which, like the sweet natural taste of unsalted butter or prawns, needs no work to achieve. In China, cooks frequently add sugar as a seasoning to try to recreate '*hsien*' in other savoury dishes.

The delicate texture of scallops demands a light hand from the cook. If cooked, they should be seared over a high heat or poached briefly over a low heat, to ensure that they remain tender and sweet inside. Searing has the added benefit of caramelization, which imbues them with a bitter note that subtly intensifies their umami sweetness. A drop of fruity sourness, for instance from citrus juice, will also amplify their inherent sweetness, as will other sweet, salty or umami foods such as sweetcorn, bacon or peas.

cream

Lick a spoonful of thick double cream and allow it to slowly dissolve in your mouth – it has an unctuous sweetness quite different from the mildly acidic French crème fraîche. This is because the lactose in British cream is no longer ripened and converted into lactic acid, unlike its Gallic counterpart. The same is true of all forms of British cream, regardless of whether they are single (20% fat content), whipping (35%), double (48%) or clotted (60%). Consequently, cream is a useful source of mild sweetness in both sweet and savoury dishes, even when simply poured over tart poached plums or stirred into a chicken fricassee.

Cream's liquid nature also ensures that it dilutes other tastes, which in turn can help to enhance their intrinsic sweetness. The sour filling in a classic lemon tart, for example, is diluted and partially sweetened by cream.

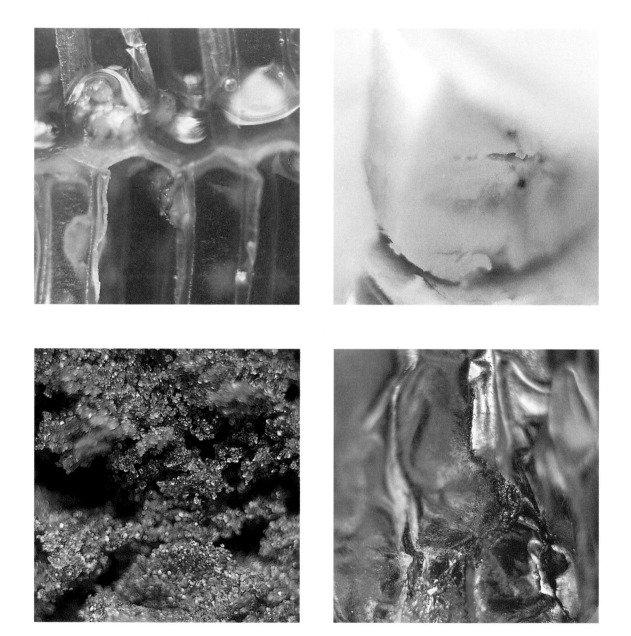

honey

The reason honey seems sweeter than sugar (sucrose) is that it is made from fructose and dextrose (glucose), and fructose tastes sweeter than sucrose although it has the same calorific value. Curiously, highly flavoured, aromatic flower honey, such as lavender or heather, tastes less sweet.

Another facet of honey is that it quickly caramelizes when subjected to heat, making it admirably suited to marinades and glazes. Duck, lamb, pork and chicken all benefit from this caramelized bitter-sweetness, as do roasted or grilled fruits such as figs or peaches. Its sticky nature also lends it to vinaigrettes. However, although honey's distinctive taste works well with other strong tastes, such as vinegar, umami soy sauce and bitter sweet nut oils, care should be taken when adding it to delicately flavoured puddings as its taste can overpower them.

sugar

The irresistible sweetness of sugar has led man astray as surely as the apple in the Garden of Eden. Today, sugar cane and sugar beet are the world's two main sources of sugar (sucrose). The former also produces unrefined brown sugars which taste less sweet and increasingly bitter (in a nice minerally way) the darker and less refined they are. The darkest is molasses sugar, followed by dark muscovado, pale muscovado, demerara, and golden unrefined caster, granulated and icing sugar.

Although the predilection for sweet-tasting food is universal, sugar's culinary use varies greatly from culture to culture, depending on how and when it was incorporated into its cooking. In Thailand, for example, sweet spiced fish is normal in a balanced savoury meal, while in India a spicy rich meal is finished with an intensely sweet, small pudding.

bananas

The sheer pleasure of eating a freshly picked banana in the tropics is hard to match. As palm leaves rustle in the sultry air, their sweet, soft flesh fills the mouth with subtle aromas. These delicate notes are lost when bananas are shipped, half-ripe, across the world. Green bananas are usually called plantain. They contain little sugar and a lot of starch, and are normally cooked in savoury dishes. Ripe bananas, however, are the opposite, with 20% sugar and 2% starch, and are best in sweet dishes, cooked or raw.

I will only be dealing with ripe dessert bananas (*Musa hybrids*). Their sweetness can be enhanced by a little sourness, for example from tamarind, soured cream, lime juice or rum. Salt, and bitter foods such as chocolate or Angostura bitters, imbue bananas with a satisfying complexity, while sweet ingredients such as coconut milk complement them.

dates

A soft date melts in the mouth like a piece of fudge. The fruit of the date palm (*Phoenix dactylifera*), the date is regarded as a staple food in the Middle East, where cooks can choose from a delectable array of red, brown and yellow varieties, each with their own subtle flavour and texture. Over 2000 varieties are cultivated in the Arabian peninsula alone. Dried dates contain up to 80% of sugar. In the West, only a few varieties of semi-dried dates are sold, normally Medjool, Deglet Noor, Hadrawi and Hayani.

The date's very sweetness makes it difficult to cook unless it is diluted by other tastes. Middle Eastern cooks excel at transforming dates into sweetmeats flavoured with nuts, butter and orange-flower water. The Moroccans have a penchant for cooking them in aromatic lamb tagines and in the West they are added to sticky puddings and cakes.

drinks

Sweetness is the first taste humans experience as we suckle our mothers' milk. From infancy to adulthood we continue to imbibe and enjoy sweet drinks, albeit moving on to more sophisticated taste combinations. From the cook's perspective, such beverages offer a good medium for experimentation.

Sourness and bitterness are natural partners in sweet drinks as they both counterbalance sweetness. A blackcurrant cordial, for example, tastes sweet rather than sour due to the level of sugar it contains, yet it is this very sourness that enlivens it. A purely sweet drink, such as a plain, lemonless rose water syrup can be very monotonous. Similarly, a bitter-sweet chocolate milkshake is far more satisfying to sip than an unflavoured sweetened milkshake.

The sourer a sweet drink is, the more refreshing it will taste, just as the more bitter it is, the more satisfying it will seem. Combine bitter, sweet and sour and you will create a satisfying and stimulating drink. Many of the best cocktails contain all three elements, as all bar flies know.

I am not aware of any salty-sweet drinks, which is hardly surprising as salt is usually only added to enhance inherent sweetness in a sour drink. If the beverage is sweet and sour, or sweet, sour and bitter, you will find that although salt deepens its taste, it also loses some of its freshness. This is not unpleasant, just different. Similarly, if salt is added to a sweet-bitter drink, it tastes more complex, but not particularly appealing.

rhubarb rose water cordial

Fruit cordials are always a fine balance between sweet and sour tastes. Here, sour rhubarb is transformed into a delicate sweet drink by the addition of a liberal quantity of white sugar. Lemon juice emphasizes the drink's sourness, while the flavour of distilled rose water deepens its sweetness to make it perfect for summer.

makes 650ml (23fl oz)

680g (1½lb) trimmed rhubarb
680g (1½lb) granulated sugar
1 lemon, juiced
a splash over a teaspoon of distilled rose water

1 Cut the rhubarb stems into 2.5cm (1-inch) chunks. Mix with the sugar in a china bowl, cover and macerate for an hour. Add 250ml (9fl oz) of water and transfer to a non-corrosive saucepan. Dissolve the sugar over a low heat, bring to the boil, then simmer, covered, for 20 minutes, or until the rhubarb disintegrates and releases its juice. Tip into a muslin jelly bag suspended over a clean bowl and leave to drip for 6 hours.

2 Return the liquid to a non-corrosive saucepan and boil vigorously for about 10 minutes. It should reduce by about 100ml (3.5fl oz). Remove from the heat, stir in the lemon juice and pour, while warm, into a sterilized bottle or jar. Once cold, add the distilled rose water, seal, shake and store in the fridge.

3 To serve, put a few ice cubes in a glass, add cordial to taste, top up with cold water or soda and stir.

tonic water

A simple way to taste a bitter-sweet drink is to pour yourself a glass of tonic water. If you wish to increase the bitterness add some Angostura bitters; if you want to add some sourness, add a few drops of either lemon or lime juice.

caribbean rum punch

Rum punch is a classic sweet-sour-bitter drink. Given such credentials, it's irresistible at parties, so be prepared for a wild time. This is Trinidadian food writer Wendy Rahamut's recipe. The ingredients are always given as a volume such as a cup, as it is easy to remember and translate the proportions into any handy container such as a glass.

makes 1.4 litres (2½ pints)

2 cups of granulated sugar
3 cups of good dark rum
1 cup of freshly squeezed lime juice
1 teaspoon Angostura bitters
½ teaspoon freshly grated nutmeg or more to taste
lime slices and maraschino cherries to garnish

1 Place the sugar and 4 cups of water in a saucepan and set over a low heat. Stir until the sugar has dissolved, then boil for 6–8 minutes. Transfer to a large jug and leave to cool.

2 Add the rum, lime juice, Angostura bitters and nutmeg to the syrup. Chill until ready for use then, if necessary, adjust to taste by adding more lime juice, water, bitters or nutmeg. You won't need more rum!

3 Fill your glasses with crushed ice, pour over the punch and garnish with lime slices and cherries.

soups

When making soups, sweetness is a useful weapon in the cook's armoury. Carefully used, sweetness is guaranteed to make people lap a soup up as a delectable dish that both comforts and satisfies. I am not referring to the old trick of adding a pinch of sugar to a tomato soup, but rather to the extraordinary array of naturally sweet foods that can be added to soup. Potatoes, parsnips, cream, carrots, sautéed onions or squash, for example, or beetroot, celeriac, fennel, avocado, rice, pulses or pasta.

The key to success is to maximize the primary taste of your chosen soup by utilizing the other tastes. Some ingredients, such as sweet potatoes, sweetcorn and red peppers, can seem too sweet and cloying when simmered in a soup unless suitably adjusted. The solution is to redress this by introducing a refreshing sour element – the most obvious is some form of soured cream, such as buttermilk, crème fraîche or yoghurt, although other sour ingredients, such as cooking apples, tamarind or sorrel, can also be used. A last minute squeeze of lime or lemon juice is also very effective.

When planning a soup that uses relatively sweet ingredients, remember that any stock you use will imbue the soup with umami. This will make the dish taste sweeter, but also more appetizing in a savoury sort of way. If you want to further emphasize its sweetness, salty foods such as ham bones or bacon are useful, as is umami-rich Parmesan cheese. Or, if you want to enhance a soup's sweetness in an intriguing way, add a bitter ingredient such as a good olive oil, rocket, watercress or even a swirl of pesto.

pea and rocket soup

Bitter rocket is added at the last minute to this sweet green soup to give an alluring depth to its sweet-umami taste of peas and chicken stock. Mildly sweet cream helps dilute the intensity without undermining the soup's sweetness. I use cultivated 'wild' rocket, as it is more peppery and bitter than ordinary rocket, but both are good.

serves 4

2 bunches of spring onions, trimmed
and roughly sliced
3 cloves of garlic, roughly diced
3 tablespoons olive oil
850ml (30fl oz) chicken stock
800g (1¾lb) shelled peas
225g (8oz) rocket
285ml (½ pint) double cream
salt and freshly ground black pepper
scant 140ml (¼ pint) double cream to serve
a handful of attractive rocket leaves to serve

1 In a large saucepan, gently fry the spring onions and garlic in the olive oil until soft. Add the chicken stock, bring to the boil, then add the peas.

2 Return to the boil, then cover and simmer gently for 20 minutes, or until the peas are very soft. Stir in the rocket and cook for a further 2–3 minutes, then immediately liquidize.

3 Add the cream and season to taste. Chill or reheat, depending on whether you wish to serve the soup cold or hot with a swirl of double cream and a few rocket leaves in the centre.

spiced parsnip soup

The intense sweetness of parsnips is lessened by the addition of sour cooking apples and crème fraîche to create a refreshing soup that can be eaten hot or cold. The spices add an alluring addictive flavour. Other sweet roots, such as beetroot, sweet potato or carrot, also taste good in soups when lightly soured with crème fraîche, soured cream or yoghurt.

serves 6

5 tablespoons sunflower oil
2 onions, diced
2 cloves of garlic, diced
1 teaspoon ground turmeric
1 teaspoon ground cumin
1 teaspoon ground ginger
½ teaspoon chilli powder
680g (1½lb) parsnips
2 large Bramley cooking apples
salt and freshly ground black pepper
285ml (½ pint) crème fraîche
a handful of fresh chives, finely sliced

1 Heat the oil in a large saucepan and gently fry the onions and garlic until soft. Add the spices and continue to fry over a low heat for 3 minutes.

2 Meanwhile, scrub clean the parsnips before slicing off their tops and tails and peeling them. Roughly dice and stir into the spiced onions, ensuring that they are well coated in the oil. Cook over a medium-low heat, stirring occasionally, for 5 minutes.

3 Peel, core and dice the apples. Mix them into the parsnips. Cover and continue to cook for 5 minutes, stirring occasionally. Add about 1 litre (1¾ pints) water, bring to the boil and season, before simmering for 30 minutes or until the parsnips are meltingly soft. Liquidize and season with salt and black pepper. If serving cold, chill covered until the soup is needed.

4 When you are ready to serve, if necessary, reheat the soup, then mix in the crème fraîche. Add a little water if you prefer a thinner soup, but once the crème fraîche is added do not let the mixture boil or it may split. Sprinkle with chives and serve chilled or piping hot.

salads

Sweetness has an important role in savoury salads, since it is linked in our minds to appetizing food. The level of sweetness varies greatly according to culture. Moroccans, for example, sometimes include very sweet salads in their meals, while the French enjoy tart salads.

Sweetness is normally added either as an integral part of the dressing or in the shape of one of the salad's composite ingredients. The former will make everything taste a little sweeter, but also deliciously refreshing as the very nature of a salad dressing is sour. The latter acts as a contrast to the other ingredients as you chew the salad. Thus, a juicy slice of pear will bring out the sweetness of bitter chicory, while the bitter chicory makes the pear taste all the sweeter. If a salad is predominately made up of sweet ingredients, the dressing needs to be more sour than usual to enliven the salad.

moroccan carrot salad

A simple, but utterly delicious, example of a sweet and sour salad, which is an adaptation of a recipe by Paula Wolfert in her book *Moroccan Cuisine*. Here, the sweet taste of carrots is intensified by the addition of sugar, salt and bitter coriander leaves, before being moderated with lemon juice. The distilled orange-flower water brings out the carrot's delicate flavour. The same principle could apply to cooked beetroot.

serves 4

8 medium carrots
4 tablespoons caster sugar
4 tablespoons lemon juice
2 teaspoons distilled orange-flower water
a pinch of salt
2 handfuls of fresh coriander leaves

1 Peel, top and tail the carrots, then roughly grate into a mixing bowl. Stir in the sugar, lemon juice, orange-flower water and salt and leave to marinate for 1 hour before serving.

2 When ready to eat, mix in the coriander leaves, then transfer to a pretty bowl.

feta, mint and green leaf salad with a honey-walnut vinaigrette

Sweetened vinaigrettes are a useful way of adding sweetness to a salad. Here, honey is combined with a bitter-sour walnut oil and lemon juice vinaigrette, which in turn underlines the bitter-sweet nature of the lettuce leaves and walnut kernels. The salty feta cheese helps reinstate the salad's savoury nature. It tastes wonderful. The same idea can be applied to a wide variety of combinations.

serves 4

1 teaspoon honey
2 tablespoons lemon juice
5 tablespoons walnut oil
salt and freshly ground black pepper
a pinch of cayenne pepper, optional
5 little gem lettuce hearts
3 spring onions, trimmed and finely sliced
a handful of fresh mint leaves
140g (5oz) good feta cheese, roughly crumbled
a handful of walnut kernels

1 Whisk together the honey, lemon juice and walnut oil. Season to taste with salt, freshly ground black pepper and cayenne pepper. Set aside.

2 Separate the lettuce leaves, discarding any tough outer leaves. Wash and spin dry, then place in a large salad bowl. Rip any particularly large leaves. Add the sliced spring onions, mint leaves, feta cheese and walnut kernels. When ready to serve, rewhisk the vinaigrette, pour on to the salad and gently mix. Serve immediately as a refreshing starter.

winter green, bacon and parsnip crisp salad

Naturally sweet roots, such as parsnips, can be made to taste even sweeter by deep-frying them as crisps and sprinkling with salt. Here their crunchy texture adds an interesting sweet contrast to the soft sweet caramelized shallots and bitter leaves. The salty bacon and sour dressing enhances this, while making it a more satisfying salad to eat. Beetroot, carrot or celeriac crisps could be used in the same way.

serves 6

255g (9oz) small shallots
6 tablespoons extra virgin olive oil
salt and freshly ground black pepper
a few sprigs of fresh thyme
1 tablespoon good sherry vinegar
1 bunch of watercress, trimmed into small sprigs
200g (7oz) mixed salad, including curly endive and radicchio
2 large parsnips
sunflower oil for deep-frying
225g (8oz) smoked back bacon, diced

1 Preheat the oven to 350°F (180°C) gas 4. Peel the shallots and toss in 1 tablespoon of olive oil. Lightly season, then place in a small roasting pan with some sprigs of thyme and cover with foil. Roast for 1 hour. The shallots should be meltingly soft and golden. If they need a little more colour, remove the foil covering for the last 10 minutes.

2 Meanwhile, measure the vinegar into a small bowl and whisk in 2 tablespoons of olive oil. Season to taste. Put the watercress and salad leaves in a large mixing bowl, cover, and chill until needed.

3 Trim and peel the parsnips. Cut into thin slices lengthways (if possible, use a mandolin) and drop them into a large bowl of cold water as you do so. Then drain and rinse under the cold tap before drying either in a salad spinner or in a clean tea-towel.

4 Heat the sunflower oil in a deep-fat fryer to 190°C (375°F). Add a batch of sliced dried parsnips and fry for about a minute, until they are golden and crisp. Remove, shake dry and toss in kitchen paper. Set aside in a large bowl and lightly salt. Repeat the process until all are cooked.

5 Heat 3 tablespoons of olive oil in a small frying pan and fry the bacon until it is crisp and golden. Remove and tip into the salad leaves. Add the warm shallots and the rewhisked vinaigrette and mix gently before carefully adding the parsnip crisps. Divide between 6 plates and serve immediately.

marinades

Sugar, like salt, has an important role in marinades. Originally it was combined with salt as an aid to preservation. Bacon and hams, for example, were frequently marinated in a salty-sweet dry cure or sweet brine before being smoked. Gravadlax, the Norwegian cured salmon, is still marinated in a sugar-salt mixture. Like salt, sugar changes the texture of such foods, drawing out excess moisture and firming up their flesh. Add too much sugar to a gravadlax and the salmon becomes candyfied. But used in moderation, sugar will enhance the natural sweetness or *'hsien'* of an ingredient.

The composition of any marinade is mainly dependent on what taste and flavours you want to emphasize in your final dish. Sweetness, whether it is added in the form of sugar, honey or mirin (a Japanese sweet rice cooking wine), will enhance the sweetness of any marinated fish and meat, as will a little of a salty, umami or sour ingredient such as soy sauce and lime juice. Always taste and, if necessary, adjust a marinade before using. Sweetness, however, has another benefit as a marinade – its sticky nature will cling to the ingredients it coats and caramelize when subjected to heat, imbuing them with a mildly bitter sweetness.

grilled honey-lime marinated squid

Sweet-sour marinades, such as this lime juice and honey version, emphasize any underlying sweet freshness in food, even when it has been pre-cooked. The same recipe can be used on freshly cooked shellfish, such as mussels, or even on grilled chicken or pigeon. It will negate some of the bloody bitterness of the latter. The addition of bitter leaves, such as watercress, always gives a sexy edge.

serves 4

2 teaspoons honey
½ small red chilli, or to taste, finely diced
finely grated zest and juice of 1 lime
1 tablespoon walnut oil
salt and freshly ground black pepper
450g (1lb) cleaned squid
1 tablespoon extra virgin olive oil
1 bunch of watercress, trimmed
1 cos lettuce heart, leaves separated and ripped

1 Mix together the honey, chilli, lime zest and juice and walnut oil. Season to taste and set aside.

2 Rinse the cleaned squid and cut up the side of each body so that you can open it out as a flat sheet. Using a sharp knife, neatly score a diamond pattern on the outside of each squid and cut into wide strips. If you are cooking the tentacles and they are large, carefully scrape off their suckers as many people find these off-putting. Pat dry and mix in 1 tablespoon of olive oil. Season with salt and pepper.

3 Preheat an oven-top grill-pan over a high heat. Once very hot, cook the squid in batches. It only takes a few seconds to cook, so as soon as it is no longer opalescent, remove and mix into the honey marinade. Leave to cool. Once tepid, add the salad leaves and arrange artistically on individual plates. Serve immediately as a starter.

sweet spiced beef with green beans

Marinating meat with a flavoured sugar and salt mixture will give it a succulent, firm texture and imbue it with a 'hsien'-like taste. In this recipe soy sauce adds umami to create an amazingly moreish dish. Try adapting this recipe to other red meats such as duck or venison. Smaller quantities need less time to marinate.

serves 4

170g (6oz) light brown muscovado sugar
155g (5½oz) coarse sea salt
1½ teaspoons ground star anise
1½ tablespoons finely chopped fresh ginger
3 cloves of garlic, finely chopped
zest of 2 lemons, finely grated
1–2 red chillies, finely sliced
115ml (4fl oz) Kikkoman soy sauce
115ml (4fl oz) toasted sesame oil
450g (1lb) trimmed fillet of beef
2 tablespoons sunflower oil

salad

340g (12oz) fine green beans, trimmed
3 red chicories
1 red onion, sliced into rings
a generous ½ teaspoon honey
1 clove of garlic, finely chopped
1 generous tablespoon lemon juice
3 tablespoons walnut oil
salt and freshly ground black pepper

1 Mix the sugar, salt, star anise, ginger, garlic, lemon zest, red chilli, soy sauce and sesame oil in a dish just large enough to fit the beef. Add the beef, thoroughly coat in its marinade, cover and place in the fridge.

2 After 12 hours, turn the meat, rubbing it all over with the spicy marinade. Leave, covered in the fridge, to marinate for up to 36 hours. Then rinse under the cold tap and pat dry.

3 Preheat the oven to 200°C (400°F) gas mark 6. Heat the sunflower oil in a non-stick frying pan. As soon as it is hot, add the beef and colour on all sides. Then transfer to a baking dish and pour over the oil from the pan. Place in the oven and roast for 12 minutes. Remove, cool and chill until needed.

4 Shortly before serving, make the salad by dropping the beans into a pan of boiling water. Cook for 6 minutes, or until tender. Drain and leave to cool. Separate and wash the chicory leaves and tear into large pieces. Place in a large bowl with the cooked beans and onion rings. Whisk together the honey, garlic, lemon juice and walnut oil. Season to taste and dress the salad. Divide between 4 plates and top with thick slices of the meat.

sauces

The easiest way to introduce sweetness into a dish is via an accompanying sauce. This also has the benefit of allowing eaters to control how much they use to accompany their food. Naturally, such sauces vary in sweetness from the mild milk-based bread sauce to the ultra-sweet toffee pudding sauce. In all cases they will enhance any intrinsic sweetness in a dish. This is because sweetness lessens sourness, bitterness and saltiness, while at the same time highlighting any other sweetness. Thus a plain white sauce will soften the bitterness of roasted endive and enhance its intrinsic sweetness, just as a sticky rum syrup will intensify the sweetness of a rum baba.

grilled scallops with pea sauce

The sweet-umami taste of peas is increased in this sauce with the umami chicken stock, and then lightened with sour crème fraîche. Here, it toys with the natural umami-sweetness of the scallops, but it could be used to enhance less sweet foods such as fish, duck or chicken.

serves 4 as a starter

3 tablespoons olive oil
1 clove of garlic, roughly chopped
170ml (6fl oz) chicken stock
200g (7oz) shelled fresh peas
2 sprigs of fresh mint
3 tablespoons crème fraîche
salt and freshly ground black pepper
a pinch of freshly grated nutmeg
12–16 fat scallops
3–4 slices smoked back bacon, cut into large dice

1 To make the pea sauce, heat 1 tablespoon of olive oil in a small saucepan and gently fry the garlic until soft. Add the stock, bring to the boil and drop in the peas and mint. Simmer gently for 20 minutes, then remove the mint and purée. Strain into a clean saucepan, stir in the crème fraîche and season to taste with salt, freshly ground black pepper and freshly grated nutmeg. Reheat when ready to serve.

2 Clean the scallops by removing the tough small white muscle attached to the girth, along with the thin black intestinal thread. Gently rinse clean and pat dry. Preheat an oven-top grill pan and small frying pan over a medium-high heat.

3 Add a tablespoon of oil and the bacon to a frying pan. Cook briskly until the bacon is crisp and golden, then transfer to some kitchen paper. Toss the scallops in 1 tablespoon of olive oil, lightly season, and cook in the oven-top grill-pan for 5–6 minutes, turning regularly.

4 Serve immediately by swirling a circle of warm pea purée on each of 4 warm plates. Divide the scallops between each plate, arranging them in the centre of the purée, and scatter with the crisp bacon.

tagliatelle and prawns with cream sauce

Cream is reduced into many sauces, adding an unctuous sweetness that echoes the sweetness of other ingredients such as pasta and prawns. Here, cream is combined with reduced fish stock and reduced wine, whose umami and sour nature adds a satisfyingly savoury dimension that is utterly gorgeous. It can be adapted to chicken stock and used with any white meat.

serves 4

16 large, whole raw tiger prawns
4 tablespoons sunflower oil
1 small fennel, roughly sliced
1 stick of celery, roughly sliced
1 carrot, peeled and roughly sliced
1 onion, roughly sliced
1 leek, roughly sliced
4 sprigs of fresh parsley
1 bay leaf
5 black peppercorns
285ml (½ pint) dry white wine
285ml (½ pint) double cream
285g (10oz) dried tagliatelle or 4 handfuls fresh green tagliatelle
½ lemon, juiced
salt and freshly ground black pepper
a small handful of fresh parsley, tarragon and chives, finely chopped

1 Rinse the prawns under the cold tap, then twist off their heads and unpeel the shells. Cover and chill the peeled bodies while you make the stock. Heat 3 tablespoons of sunflower oil in a wide saucepan. Briskly fry the heads and shells until they turn pink. Add the sliced vegetables and continue to sauté for 3–4 minutes, until soft. Then add the parsley, bay leaf, peppercorns, 140ml (¼ pint) wine and 2 litres (3½ pints) cold water.

2 Bring up to the boil, skim off any froth, then, as soon as it begins to boil, lower the heat and gently simmer for 25 minutes. Strain into a clean saucepan and return to the boil. Bubble vigorously until it has reduced by two-thirds. Add the remaining white wine and continue to boil until it has reduced by half. Stir in the cream and boil until it forms a creamy, delicious-tasting sauce. This is best made in advance as it takes some time.

3 Clean the prawns by making a small incision down the length of the back and removing the dark digestive cord. Rinse clean, pat dry on kitchen paper and set aside.

4 Cook the pasta according to the packet instructions, until it is *al dente*. Meanwhile, heat 1 tablespoon of sunflower oil in a non-stick frying pan over a medium-high heat. Stir-fry the prawns for 3 minutes, or until they turn pink. Add the lemon juice, season with freshly ground black pepper, then add the chopped herbs and a little of the sauce. Drain the pasta, toss in the rest of the cream sauce and divide between 4 plates. Add the prawns with their sauce and serve immediately.

chicken satay with peanut sauce

The sugar and sour lime juice in this recipe subtly increases the natural sweetness of the bitter-sweet roasted peanuts. Umami and salt are added with the fish sauce (nam pla). Such a combination will enhance the natural sweetness of everything from prawns and pork to rice and beef.

serves 4

chicken satay

2 stems of lemon grass, finely chopped
1 red chilli, finely chopped
1 clove of garlic, finely chopped
1 shallot, finely chopped
1 tablespoon fish sauce (nam pla)
2 tablespoons lime juice
1 tablespoon dark muscovado sugar
1 tablespoon sunflower oil
370g (13oz) chicken breast, cut into thin strips

peanut sauce

8 tablespoons crunchy peanut butter
1 shallot, finely chopped
2 stems of lemon grass, finely chopped
285ml (½ pint) canned coconut milk
1 red chilli, finely chopped
1 tablespoon dark muscovado sugar
1 tablespoon fish sauce (nam pla)
1 lime, juiced
a handful of fresh coriander leaves

1 Mix together all the satay ingredients except for the chicken. Thread the chicken on to wooden skewers, place in a shallow dish and coat in the satay marinade. Cover and chill for up to 1 hour, turning occasionally.

2 Meanwhile, place all the ingredients for the peanut sauce (apart from the lime juice and coriander) in a small saucepan and set over a low heat. Stir until the peanut butter has dissolved, then simmer gently until the mixture has thickened. Stir regularly to prevent it sticking; it will thicken as it cools. Mix in the lime juice and remove from the heat.

3 Preheat an oven-top grill-pan over a high heat. Grill the chicken for about 2 minutes on each side. Serve with the warm or tepid peanut sauce, garnished with the coriander leaves.

savoury dishes

Sweetness is key in bringing out the natural taste or 'hsien' of food. Whatever ingredient you use, always analyze its sweetness before deciding whether to subtly enhance or lessen it. A hint of sourness, saltiness, umami and bitterness, for example, will increase it, while a liberal dash will reduce it. Similarly, certain aromatic flavourings can also enhance our perception of sweetness, as can be discovered in chapter 6 (Flavours). The following recipes use naturally very sweet foods, which you may choose to balance with a refreshing salty-sour dish such as a relish or salad.

stir-fried scallops with sugar snap peas

This recipe tastes intense because of the dominance of umami and sweetness in the scallops, sugar snap peas and shiitake mushrooms. A pinch of salt and soy sauce underline this further. The idea can be adapted to similar-tasting foods, such as prawns, lobster and crab, as well as to peas and bitter-sweet asparagus.

serves 2

1 scant teaspoon cornflour
1 tablespoon egg white
6-8 large scallops, without their roe
3 spring onions, trimmed
4 thin slices of fresh root ginger, finely shredded
4 tablespoons sunflower oil
140g (5oz) sugar snap peas, topped and tailed
55g (2oz) shiitake mushrooms, ripped into chunks
2 tablespoons sake
salt
1 teaspoon soy sauce, optional

1 Beat the cornflower into the egg white with a fork. Clean the scallops by removing the small tough white muscle on their girth and any dark digestive cord. Rinse, pat dry and cut into quarters. Then coat in the beaten egg white mixture.

2 Finely slice the spring onions, separating the green tops from the white stems. Mix the ginger into the latter. Bring a saucepan of salted water to the boil, and add 1 tablespoon of sunflower oil and the sugar snap peas. Cook for 30 seconds and drain immediately.

3 Heat 3 tablespoons of sunflower oil in a wok or frying pan. Add the ginger mix, sizzle for a few seconds, then add the scallops and stir-fry briskly for 20 seconds before adding the mushrooms. Stir-fry briskly, then mix in the sake, sugar snap peas and green spring onion tops. Season to taste with salt or soy sauce and serve piping hot with steamed rice and chilli sauce.

sugar-baked ham

Sugar and honey are a useful means of adding a wonderful bitter sweet note to roast meat. Here, the former is mixed with bitter mustard powder and flavourings to make a caramelized glaze for roast ham. The salty nature of the ham intensifies the taste of the glaze, while the glaze enhances the sweetness in the ham.

serves 8

1.8kg (4lb) gammon
2 large carrots, peeled and roughly sliced
2 onions, quartered
1 small celeriac, peeled and roughly chopped
1 bay leaf, with a few sprigs of fresh parsley and thyme
4 black peppercorns
cloves
2 tablespoons runny honey
55g (2oz) light brown muscovado sugar
2 teaspoons English mustard powder
1 teaspoon ground cinnamon
½ teaspoon cayenne pepper

1 Place the gammon in a large saucepan with the vegetables, herbs and peppercorns. Cover with cold water. Bring slowly to the boil, skim off any scum, and simmer gently for 1 hour, topping up with water if necessary. Remove from the heat and leave to cool.

2 Preheat the oven to 180°C (350°F) gas mark 4. Cut away the meat rind. Score the fat into diamonds and stud with cloves. Wrap in greaseproof paper, then tightly wrap in foil and place in a roasting tin. Bake for 30 minutes, then remove. Increase the oven heat to 220°C (425°F) gas mark 7. Slowly melt the honey, sugar, mustard, cinnamon and cayenne in a saucepan. Open the gammon package, expose the fat and liberally coat with spice. Bake uncovered for 30 minutes.

risotto with peas and bacon

Sweetness, umami and salt can produce a satisfying dish. In this recipe sweet-tasting peas and rice are combined with salty bacon, umami stock and Parmesan. Try squeezing lemon juice over it to test the effect of sourness.

serves 4

3 tablespoons olive oil
225g (8oz) smoked back bacon, finely diced
1 onion, finely chopped
1 clove of garlic, finely chopped
1.1 litres (2 pints) good chicken stock
900g (2lb) (unshelled weight) peas, shelled
30g (1oz) butter
310g (11oz) risotto rice, such as Arborio or Carnaroli
15g (½oz) Parmesan cheese, freshly grated
salt and freshly ground black pepper

1 Put the oil in a wide saucepan and fry the bacon until it begins to colour. Add the onion and garlic and cook until soft. Divide the stock between 2 pans and bring to the boil. Add half the peas to one, return to the boil, cover and simmer for 10 minutes. Add the butter to the bacon and mix in the raw peas. Cook for 2 minutes, then stir in the rice. Fry for 2 minutes. Mix in 2–3 ladles of the plain hot stock. Stir, adding stock as it's absorbed.

2 Liquidize the peas with their cooking broth. Once you have used up the plain stock, slowly add the green pea broth to the rice. After 18–24 minutes, all the stock will have been absorbed and the rice should be fluffy with a slight bite. Stir in the Parmesan and season.

lamb and date tagine

Middle Eastern cooking often includes sweet dried or semi-dried fruits in dishes with spiced meat. The fruits emphasize the natural sweetness in the meat. In this recipe, saffron adds a faint bitter note which, in conjunction with the salt, underlines the sweet-savoury nature of the dish. A last minute squeeze of lemon juice acts as a refreshing counterbalance.

serves 4

1kg (2lb 3oz) lean lamb, diced
a large pinch of saffron stamens
1 teaspoon salt
a generous pinch of freshly ground black pepper
1 teaspoon ground ginger
½ teaspoon cayenne pepper
2 cloves of garlic, finely chopped
3 tablespoons olive oil
a small bunch of fresh coriander, finely chopped
a small bunch of fresh parsley, finely chopped
30g (1oz) butter
340g (12oz) onions, finely diced
140g (5oz) Medjool dates, stoned
a pinch of ground cinnamon
1 lemon, quartered

1 Trim the meat of excess fat and cut into 3cm (1¼ inch) chunks. Place in a large saucepan. Grind the saffron with the salt under a teaspoon until it forms a fine powder. Add the freshly ground black pepper, ginger and cayenne pepper, then rub into the meat with the garlic and oil.

2 Add the herbs, cold butter and half the onions. Set over a medium-high heat and stir regularly until the lamb is lightly coloured. Stir in 710ml (1¼ pints) water, bring to the boil, then reduce to a simmer. Cook very gently, uncovered, for an hour. Then add the remaining diced onions and simmer for 50 minutes, or until very tender. Adjust the seasoning to taste.

3 Meanwhile, preheat the oven to its highest setting. Stone and quarter the dates. Transfer the stew to an ovenproof serving dish. Arrange the dates among the meat and sprinkle them with a little cinnamon. Bake for 5-10 minutes, or until the dates look crusty. Serve immediately with lemon wedges and rice or couscous.

puddings and cakes

Puddings, cakes and sweets were created as a luxurious indulgence to satisfy our innate craving for sweetness. In virtually every culture, some form of sweetmeat is served to guests as a treat. No doubt this custom grew from the fact that our appetite is still primarily for sweet foods and, aside from the sheer pleasure of eating such delicacies, they also leave us feeling replete.

As a dominant taste, sweetness needs to be controlled; an over-sweet pudding can be sickly if not carefully balanced by sourness, saltiness and/or bitterness. Much depends on whether you wish to create a refreshing or a satisfying pudding. The former is achieved by adding sourness, the latter by adding bitterness – but be careful, as too cautious a hand will merely make the dish taste even sweeter. Salt can also emphasize sweetness, but it has the added benefit of giving a subtle, savoury depth to a recipe, which is useful when seeking a sophisticated sweet taste.

Sweetness alters the texture of food. Honey, golden syrup and dark unrefined sugars, for example, add a moist stickiness to cakes and puddings; as do very sweet fruits such as bananas, dates and dried fruits. Refined white sugars, when combined with whisked egg white, introduce a fragile sweet airiness to mousses, soufflés, roulades and meringues which literally melts in the mouth. Even sweet syrups drenched over cakes, sponge puddings and fresh fruit imbue them with succulent stickiness.

sugared almond cakes

Cakes are among the subtlest of sweet foods, with their alluring mixture of naturally sweet butter, eggs, flour and, of course, sugar. In this recipe, a hint of bitterness has been added via the almonds and almond essence, which make these cakes particularly satisfying to eat. A final crunchy sprinkling of sugar over the cakes merely adds an even sweeter contrast. These work well if baked in a muffin mould.

makes 8

115g (4oz) unsalted butter, softened, plus extra for buttering
150g (5¼oz) caster sugar, plus extra for dusting
3 medium eggs
85g (3oz) ground almonds
45g (1¾oz) plain flour, sifted
a few drops of natural almond essence

1 Preheat the oven to 180°C (350°F) gas mark 4 and liberally butter the muffin moulds.

2 Beat the butter until pale, then gradually add the sugar, beating all the time. Once pale, continue by beating in each egg, then fold in the almonds followed by the sifted flour. Finally, mix in the almond essence. Spoon into 8 muffin moulds and bake for 18 minutes, or until springy and golden. Turn out on to a cooling rack and dust liberally with caster sugar.

lavender panna cotta

The most subtle of flavourings will enhance the wonderful light sweetness of milk and cream. Lavender, for example, imbues them with a magical fresh note. This panna cotta is accompanied by fresh raspberries, whose sweet-sourness further emphasizes the dish's intrinsic fresh sweetness. You will need 5 small dariole moulds, about 150ml (5fl oz) capacity, for this recipe.

serves 5

4 sprigs of fresh lavender flowers
565ml (1 pint) double cream
140ml (5fl oz) full-fat milk
3 sheets of leaf gelatine
140g (5oz) caster sugar
2 tablespoons peach liqueur or good white dessert wine
sunflower oil for greasing
340g (12oz) fresh raspberries

1 Gently rinse the fresh lavender sprigs and place in a large saucepan with the cream and milk. Stir and set over a medium-low heat. Once it begins to come up to the boil, reduce the temperature to allow it to gently but steadily bubble until it has reduced by about approximately one-third.

2 Meanwhile, soak the gelatine sheets in a bowl of cold water for about 5 minutes. Once they are floppy, drain and gently squeeze out the excess water.

3 Strain the hot cream into a clean bowl and stir in the gelatine and sugar until both have dissolved. Then add the peach liqueur or dessert wine.

4 Very lightly oil the dariole moulds, then pour in the panna cotta mixture. Chill until set. When ready to serve, gently pull the side of each panna cotta away from the mould before inverting it on to a plate, then give a sharp shake to release it. Accompany with a scattering of fresh raspberries.

banana flambé

Frying, grilling and roasting all intensify naturally sweet ingredients such as bananas. A generous dash of acidic citrus juice will lighten their sweetness, while bitter-sweet alcohol will add a satisfying bitter note that resonates with the bitter-sweet caramelized fruit. This can easily be adapted to other sweet fruits, such as figs or pears.

serves 4

4 large bananas, peeled
30g (1oz) butter
pinch of cinnamon
30g (1oz) demerara sugar
½ lemon, juiced
½ orange, juiced
3 tablespoons dark rum

1 Quarter the bananas by halving their length before cutting them in half lengthways. Melt the butter in a non-stick frying pan over a medium heat. Add the bananas, cut-side-down, and fry briskly for a minute, before flipping them over and stirring in the cinnamon and sugar. Fry for a minute, then pour in the juices. Shake the pan and allow to boil for a few minutes.

2 As soon as the bananas look cooked and the sauce has thickened slightly, remove from the heat and pour over the rum. Quickly set alight, shaking the pan slightly to ensure the alcohol burns off. Serve immediately.

walnut whisky tart

Whisky adds a subtle bitterness to the bitter-sweet walnuts that helps satiate the appetite.

serves 6

225g (8oz) shortcrust pastry (see page 203)
200g (7oz) walnut kernels, roughly broken
200m (7fl oz) double cream
155g (5½oz) granulated sugar
pinch of salt
2 tablespoons whisky
icing sugar for dusting

1 Roll out the pastry on a lightly floured surface and line a 23cm (9-inch) tart dish. Prick the bottom with a fork, line with baking paper and fill with baking beans. Chill for 30 minutes. Preheat the oven to 200°C (400°F) gas mark 6. Place the tart in the oven and bake blind for 15 minutes. Remove from the oven, lift out the paper and baking beans and lower the temperature to 180°C (350°F) gas mark 4.

2 Meanwhile, put the walnuts, cream, sugar, salt and whisky in a saucepan. Set over a low heat and stir until the sugar has dissolved, then simmer until the mixture thickens slightly and turns a pale gold (this will take about 15–20 minutes). Allow to cool slightly, then pour into the partially-cooked pastry case. Return to the oven. Bake for 20 minutes, turning occasionally to ensure it cooks evenly. It will not fully set until after it is cold. Serve cold with soured cream, dusted with icing sugar.

sticky date pudding with toffee sauce

This is another bitter-sweet variation. Ultra-sweet, semi-dried dates are steamed in a moist sponge pudding with mildly bitter tea and unrefined sugar. They are then served with a very sweet and mildly bitter toffee sauce, much to the satisfaction of the eater. The sauce adds a striking dimension to the pudding, making it even more tempting. You will need a 1 litre (1¾ pint) pudding basin for this.

serves 6

date pudding

170g (6oz) stoned Medjool dates, finely chopped
120ml (scant 4.5fl oz) very hot tea such as Earl Grey
85g (3oz) softened butter, plus extra for greasing pudding basin
140g (5oz) soft light muscovado sugar
½ teaspoon vanilla essence
2 large eggs
170g (6oz) self-raising flour

toffee sauce

200g (7oz) soft light muscovado sugar
6 tablespoons double cream
115g (4oz) butter

1 Place the chopped dates in a small bowl and cover with the piping hot tea. Cut two circles of greaseproof paper to fit the base and top of your pudding basin. Liberally butter the basin and line with the smaller circle of paper. Find a covered saucepan that will comfortably hold the pudding basin and fill with enough water to reach two-thirds of the way up the basin. Remove the basin and bring the water to the boil.

2 Beat together the butter and sugar. Add the vanilla essence and then the eggs. Finally, beat in the flour, followed by the dates and tea. Spoon into the buttered pudding basin. Gently press on the remaining circle of paper. Take a sheet of foil and fold in a pleat down the centre to allow the pudding to rise, then tightly wrap across the top of the pudding.

3 Lower the basin into the boiling pan of water, cover and boil steadily for 1½–2 hours or until firm. You can test to see if it is cooked by inserting a skewer or knife – if it comes out clean the pudding is ready. You will have to regularly top up with extra boiling water as the pudding cooks. Remove the basin from the saucepan, lift off the foil, peel away the greaseproof paper, and loosen the pudding with a knife before turning out on to a plate.

4 While the pudding is cooking, make the sauce. Place the light muscovado sugar, cream and butter in a saucepan and set over a low heat, stirring occasionally, until the sugar has dissolved and the butter melted. Then bring to the boil and simmer for 3 minutes. Pour over the hot pudding and serve.

preserves

Sugar is an important element in preserving fruit in jams, jellies, cheeses and syrups. It has two uses: first, it inhibits the growth of bacteria, and second, it affects the setting quality of fruit as it works in conjunction with the fruit's pectin and acid. Too little sugar will result in a poor set and the growth of mould, while too much sugar destroys the flavour of the fruit. The less the fruit is boiled with the sugar, the fresher it will taste.

apple cheese

'Fruit butter' or 'fruit cheese' is cooked, strained fruit pulp which is then boiled with sugar until it sets to a soft (butter) or firm (cheese) texture. It can be with made with damsons, plums and quinces and improves with age, provided it is stored in a cool, dark place. Traditionally, it is potted in straight-sided jars. All fruit cheeses can be served as part of a dessert with fruit and nuts, or as part of a starter with cheese or air-dried ham.

makes 850g (1lb 14oz)

850ml (1½ pints) cider
4 finely pared strips of lemon peel
4 cloves
1 small stick of cinnamon
1.4kg (3lb) cooking apples, such as Bramley's
sunflower oil
granulated sugar

1 Place the cider, lemon peel, cloves and cinnamon in a non-corrosive saucepan and boil vigorously until the cider has reduced by one-third. Roughly chop the apples, pips, skin and all, add to the pan, mix well and simmer for about 1½ hours, or until the apples are reduced to a pap.

2 Wash your glass containers and leave to dry in a very low oven. Lightly oil them with sunflower oil and set aside. Push the apples with their juice through a fine sieve. Measure out the purée and allow 340g (12oz) of sugar to each 565ml (1 pint) of apple purée.

3 Place the sugar and apple purée in a heavy-bottomed saucepan over a low heat. Stir until the sugar has dissolved, then bring to the boil and continue to cook, stirring all the time, until the mixture is so thick that the spoon leaves a clean line when drawn across the bottom of the pan. This process will take about 25 minutes and as the purée thickens it will turn a beautiful dark amber. It will also spit ferociously, so keep your arms well covered.

4 Carefully spoon the hot apple cheese into your pots. Press a small waxed disc, waxed-side-down, on to the cheese and, once cold, seal, label and date.

sweet notes

Baked, mashed or puréed sweet root vegetables, such as sweet potatoes, carrots, parsnips, celeriac and beetroot, will bring a delicate sweetness to a savoury meal regardless of whether it is a subtle starter of seared fish or a rich main course of game pie or roast meat. Try buttered baked sweet potatoes with a spicy lamb chilli – the sweet, umami, sour and salty tastes will buzz around your mouth with the chilli.

Unsalted butter sweetened with sugar (white or brown) and flavoured with citrus zest and juice and distilled flower water or spices, is a delicious way to add sweetness to pancakes and baked fruit such as apples, apricots and peaches. Either spread the flavoured butter on to cold pancakes, then fold, sprinkle with icing sugar and reheat under the grill, or lightly butter a baking dish, stuff the prepared fruit with the sweetened butter, and bake until tender and oozing with fragrant sweet juices.

Tart fruit can be transformed into a buttery, sweet pudding by being baked with a crumble topping. This tastes even better with the bitter-sweet addition of nuts. Mix your chosen fruit with lots of sugar and place in a pie dish. Then process 170g (6oz) of plain flour with 55g (2oz) of whole unblanched hazelnuts until they form fine crumbs. Add 115g (4oz) of diced semi-frozen butter and whizz for 2 minutes, again until it forms fine crumbs. Mix in 55g (2oz) of unrefined caster sugar and gently but evenly press over the top of your fruit. Bake in a preheated oven at 200°C (400°F) gas mark 6 for 10 minutes, then reduce the heat to 190°C (375°F) gas mark 5. Bake for a further 20–25 minutes. Serve hot, warm or cold.

A sweet note can be added to leafy summer salads by mixing in lightly poached sweet vegetables such as fresh peas, baby carrots or baby beetroot.

Summer fruit can be sweetened with a dash of dessert wine or sweet liqueur such as Cointreau or Crème de Cassis. Try mixing strawberries, raspberries and redcurrants with a generous few shots of Cassis for an aromatic sweet-sour pudding, or nectarines, raspberries and blueberries with Grand Marnier for a faintly bitter-sweet-sour salad.

Cream or home-made custard (see p.201) will dilute and sweeten any slightly sour pudding such as gooseberry pie. Double cream can also be sweetened, but if you want to be ultra-suave, add an appropriate eau-de-vie such as Poire William or framboise to give it a kick.

Slices of fresh apple, pineapple or banana can be lightly dusted with icing sugar before being grilled to give them a delicious bitter-sweet taste. The sugar caramelizes as the fruit cooks. Heavenly eaten with crème fraîche.

Honey, maple syrup or golden syrup can be drizzled on to food to give it an intensely sweet note. This is particularly good with sour buttermilk pancakes, which are made by sifting 285g (10oz) plain flour with ½ teaspoon salt, ½ teaspoon bicarbonate of soda and 2 teaspoons baking powder into a large mixing bowl. Make a well in the centre of the flour and gradually beat in a large egg and a tablespoon of melted butter, followed by 485ml (16fl oz) buttermilk. Once it forms a smooth batter, drop 3–4 spoonfuls on to a pre-heated well-oiled heavy frying pan. Cook over a medium heat until they are puffy with little bubbles, then flip them over and fry until golden. Repeat until the batter is finished.

Honey can also be mixed with lemon juice and drizzled over cooked semolina cakes, or brushed on to whole figs before baking for a gorgeous sticky, sweet glaze.

chilli

Chillies possess magical properties for the cook. They belong to the capsicum family and once ripe, taste sweet. There are some 200 varieties, all of which vary greatly in shape, size, heat and flavour. But their mysterious powers stem from their heat, which comes from capsaicin, an odourless, tasteless, irritant alkaloid. It is this that heightens our sense of taste, flavour and texture by exciting the palate, which in turn makes every chilli-flavoured mouthful taste interesting from first bite to last gulp.

Eaten in moderation, capsaicin also whets the appetite and aids digestion. It certainly promotes the production of endorphins, the body's natural painkillers, which stimulate that delicious sense of pleasure and well-being familiar to all chilli enthusiasts. The key to cooking with chilli is restraint, particularly as the more chilli you eat, the less sensitive you become to its heat. A hint of it will make everything from a cheese straw to a fruit salad taste more intense, regardless of whether it is sour, salty, umami, bitter or sweet. Sweetness, however, can ameliorate mild chilli heat to an exciting tingle in the mouth, while bringing out the chilli's inherent flavour – perfect for sorbets and aromatic sugar-syrups.

Since capsaicin stimulates the appetite, its inclusion in nibbles and starters will make them all the more delectable. Combine this with its enhancement of flavour, and its inclusion in savoury dishes will help you to avoid the dreaded dull main course, since the capsaicin will tease the eater into taking one alluring bite after another. Try to match the flavour of your chilli with your recipe. Smoky sweet paprika in a lemon-honey marinade for grilled chicken, for example, resonates with the smoky sweet taste of the cooked bird.

Although scientists measure the different capsaicinoid levels in chillies in Scoville Heat Units, a sophisticated analytical system, cooks will find common sense and a cautious hand more helpful. In essence, the Scoville system refers to the number of times that extracts of chillies dissolved in alcohol can be diluted with sugar water before the capsaicin can no longer be tasted. Bell peppers, for example, can range from 0 to 600, while habañeros average between 80,000 and 150,000 Scoville Heat Units. Strangely, even chillies from the same plant can vary in heat.

A chilli's heat can be lessened by removing its white ribs and seeds, as these contain up to 80% of the capsaicin. Take care, however, never to rub any part of your body when you are handling fresh or dried chillies as you can get a chilli burn, and always scrub your hands and equipment clean immediately after handling chillies. If you are fearful of an allergic reaction, you should wear rubber gloves. It is then a question of experimenting with the myriad different varieties of chillies to subtly enhance your food.

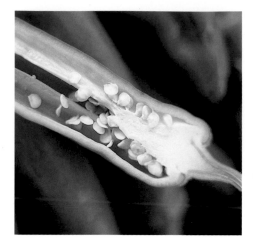

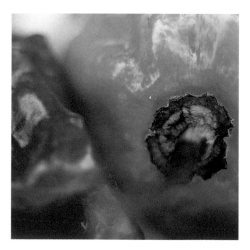

dried kashmiri chillies

Wrinkly, dried Kashmiri chillies have the look of a chilli pepper that has been hung out to dry in icy cold mountain winds. Deep red, they have a gentle heat, sweet taste and smoky aroma that is perfect for first-time chilli cooks. Like all dried chillies, their aromatic flavour will be enhanced by a light roasting in the oven or in a warm pan, before adding to a dish – they are ready when soft and aromatic; do not burn or they will taste bitter. Kashmiri chillies combine well with other spices and can be used whole, ground or soaked. Their prickly heat is delicious in sweet and savoury dishes. Tamarind, lemon and yoghurt bring out their sweetness.

thai chillies

Small, thin, elongated and pointed, Thai chillies are hot, with a clean, fresh flavour. Their juicy flesh and ultra-hot white seeds lend themselves to sweet and sour tasting food, giving it an added kick. Always add Thai chillies cautiously though, as they can vary in heat from 30,000 to 100,000 Scoville Heat Units. Use simply, rather than with myriad spices. Thai chillies seem to intensify the umami nature of soy and fish sauce, for example, in a honey and soy-dressed noodle salad or Thai-style stir-fried beef. Thai chillies also add a refreshing hot note to marinades and dips. Rice or coconut is the perfect antidote to their heat.

paprika

In Europe, dried, ground paprika comes from different varieties of paprika peppers. Spanish paprika (pimentón), for example, is lighter coloured and less fruity than the equally good Hungarian paprika. Both are sold in sweet (mild), semi-sweet and hot forms, as well as smoked and unsmoked. All have a natural pungency that makes the mouth water when eating, as can be experienced by munching any form of Spanish chorizo sausage. Paprika has an affinity with tomatoes, pulses, soured cream and yoghurt, as well as with meat, fowl and fish. It adds a flavoursome depth to grilled food.

fresh anaheim chillies

Anaheim (New Mexican) chillies range from the very mild to slightly hot, which makes them popular in salads and chillies (as in stews). They have a fresh, almost mineral-like flavour, which is deepened and sweetened if they are grilled and peeled. Prepared like this, they taste particularly good with chillied meat, as they enhance the sweet richness of the stewed, spiced meat. Anaheim chillies are usually sold green and vary in size. Larger specimens are good halved, blanched and stuffed, while smaller ones can be sliced raw for piquant pizzas. Anaheim chillies taste good with tomatoes and salty cheese regardless of how they are prepared.

cayenne pepper

There are several varieties of cayenne pepper, but all are hot, ranging from 30,000 to 50,000 Scoville Heat Units. They are normally picked when red, then dried and sold either as flakes or ground powder. They are also popular in fiery sauces, such as that from Louisiana in North America. Traditionally, cayenne pepper is added as a last minute gastronomical spike to relatively sweet food, such as scrambled eggs and béchamel sauce, and salty-sweet-umami dishes, such as cheese sauce, dressed crab and potted fish. The heat sharpens the appetite, making it all the more appreciative of the contrasting tastes.

fresh habañero

Like all chillies, habañeros go under many names, including Scotch bonnet, Congo pepper and goat pepper. Shaped like miniature crumpled Chinese lanterns, they ripen from green to white, yellow, orange and red. They look so pretty it's impossible not to be tempted to buy them, but beware, they're among the hottest of chillies. Always begin by adding a small amount, or by infusing until the liquid tastes pleasantly spicy. If used cautiously, you will discover a wonderful fruity aroma beneath their heat, which works well with fruit, fish, citrus juice and vegetables, such as in a sea bass ceviche or avocado salsa.

drinks

Surprising as it might seem, a small amount of chilli added to a cooling drink is very refreshing. It stimulates the appetite, which in a hot climate is often dulled by the heat, and heightens awareness of the other tastes and flavours in the drink. Some even favour spicing their alcohol with chilli, regardless of whether it is beer or vodka.

indian tamarind drink

This is a very refreshing sour salty drink that is an acquired taste. In Northern India, mothers make it to indulge their spice-loving sons. The salt enhances the sweetness of the tamarind, while the chilli heightens the drinker's awareness of its spicy, fruity flavour and compels you to sip more.

serves 2

55g (2oz) tamarind pulp (with seeds)
½ teaspoon chilli powder or to taste
½ teaspoon garam masala
a pinch of ground ginger
1 teaspoon caraway seeds, ground
½ teaspoon salt or to taste
a sprinkling of finely chopped fresh coriander, optional

1 Place the tamarind in a non-corrosive bowl and cover with 285ml (½ pint) of warm water. Leave for 1 hour, then rub the fruit with your fingers so that all the pulp comes away from the stones.

2 Mix in a further 285ml (½ pint) of warm water and pour through a coarse sieve into a jug. Discard the stones and the fibre.

3 Mix in the spices and salt, then chill for a minimum of 2 hours. Serve cold, sprinkled with fresh coriander.

soups

Fresh and dried chillies imbue soup with different flavours. The former are fresh and light, while the latter are more complex and aromatic. As with all dishes, chillies heighten our perception of both taste and flavour, but in the case of soup it is important to consider the texture of the soup you are spicing. If, for example, it is puréed, a light hand is needed, as there is no unspiced textural element to dilute its heat. Clear soups are a different matter, as they usually contain an element such as wontons, tofu or poached meat, that contrasts and therefore dilutes the spiciness of the broth in the mouth (see p.93). Chunky soups fall between the two.

black bean soup

Here, dried chillies are combined with an essentially sweet and salty soup to enliven its taste. However, just as a sour element (in this case the crème fraîche) is added to enhance the sweet nature of the soup, so another form of chilli, such as paprika or cayenne, can be used to emphasize its spiciness. Try with other 'sweet' soups, such as spiced sweet potato or pumpkin soup.

serves 6

500g (1lb 2oz) dried black beans
2 bunches of fresh coriander
4–5 tablespoons sunflower oil
4 onions, roughly diced
6 sticks of celery, roughly diced
4 cloves of garlic, roughly chopped
2 teaspoons ground cumin
4 dried Kashmiri chillies
2 small bay leaves
6 sprigs of fresh parsley
salt and freshly ground black pepper
140ml (¼ pint) crème fraîche or soured cream
pinch of cayenne pepper or smoked paprika

1 Soak the beans overnight. The next day, pick the coriander leaves from their stems, roughly chop the stems and store the leaves in a sealed plastic bag in the fridge. Heat the oil in a large pan and gently fry the chopped coriander stems, onions, celery and garlic until soft. Add the cumin and Kashmiri chillies and cook for 2 minutes.

2 Drain the beans and add to the pan with 2 litres (3½ pints) of cold water, the bay leaves and parsley. Bring to the boil, then boil vigorously for 10 minutes. Skim off any scum and simmer for a further 2 hours, or until the beans are very soft. Never add salt before the beans are soft, as it gives them a tough skin. Liquidize and season to taste.

3 Reheat before serving, then ladle into bowls and add a swirl of crème fraîche or soured cream. Sprinkle with cayenne pepper or smoked paprika and the coriander leaves, and serve.

salads

Chillies are ideally suited to salads, as they sharpen the appetite and set the mouth watering in anticipation of the next dish. Caution, however, is needed when adding such heat, as sensitivity varies from one person to another. The more chillies you eat, the greater your tolerance of their heat and appreciation of their different flavours. Luckily, there are many ways to add a subtle warmth to a salad, ranging from the all-pervasive heat of an infused vinegar or oil, to the addition of a spicy ingredient such as chilli olives, chorizo or spiced shellfish (see p.96). Fresh chillies should be chosen for their flavour as much as for their heat. Fruity habañeros, for example, add an aromatic fire, whereas Thai chillies give a clean, fresh heat.

An acidic salad dressing will enhance your perception of heat, while the heat itself will heighten your awareness of the salad's texture. One exception to this is creamy dressings, such as mayonnaise or yoghurt, whose unctuous nature counteracts the heat by soothing the mouth.

thai salad

The fresh hot flavour of Thai chillies is perfect for a spicy, refreshing salad that makes the taste buds tingle and has you reaching for a soothing drink. Its hot-sour nature makes you acutely aware of the crunchy texture of each ingredient as it bursts in your mouth. Try serving it as a cold accompaniment to fish or meat, preferably with something that will lessen the heat such as steamed rice. It can be adapted to other crunchy vegetables.

serves 6

2 carrots, peeled
½ mouli (or jicama), peeled or 2 bunches of radishes, trimmed but not peeled
¼ small green cabbage, shredded
2 small pak choi, shredded
½ red onion, finely sliced
2 tablespoons fish sauce (nam pla)
2 tablespoons lime juice
1 tablespoon palm sugar or light brown muscovado sugar
1 Thai chilli, finely sliced or to taste
a handful of fresh coriander leaves

1 Cut the carrots and mouli (or jicama or radishes) into thin matchsticks. Place in a mixing bowl with the shredded cabbage, pak choi and red onion.

2 Mix together the fish sauce, lime juice, sugar and chilli. This is a spicy salad, so if you are timid of chilli, add less — you can always add more later.

3 Pour the dressing over the salad, add the coriander leaves (reserving a few to garnish) and toss. Serve garnished with the remaining coriander leaves.

green salad with broad beans and chilli vinegar

A chilli vinaigrette is used in this salad to enliven the bitter-sweet taste of the broad beans and lettuce, but you could use the vinaigrette in a wide variety of simple salads, such as with beetroot and cucumber. To make chilli vinegar, slip a few fresh medium-hot chillies, such as jalapeños, into a new bottle of white wine vinegar, seal and store in a cool, dark place for 3–4 weeks before use.

serves 6

225g (8oz) shelled small broad beans
1 teaspoon chilli vinegar
2 teaspoons white wine vinegar
a large pinch of chopped fresh tarragon leaves
3 tablespoons extra virgin olive oil
salt and freshly ground black pepper
6 little gem lettuce hearts, trimmed
6 spring onions, trimmed and finely sliced

1 Drop the broad beans into a pan of boiling water and cook for 4 minutes, or until tender. Drain and cool under the cold tap, then pat dry with kitchen paper.

2 Whisk together the chilli and white wine vinegars, tarragon and olive oil. Season to taste and dress the beans. Roughly rip the lettuce leaves and add to the beans with the finely sliced spring onions. Toss and serve immediately.

chorizo, new potato and roasted pepper salad

One subtle way of imbuing a dish with the spicy heat of chilli is to add a spicy hot ingredient such as roasted Anaheim chillies or paprika-flavoured chorizo. In this recipe, both are used to enhance the earthy sweetness and succulent waxy texture of the potatoes and peppers. It makes a gorgeous lunch.

serves 4

2 large Anaheim chillies
2 red or yellow peppers, quartered and seeded
600g (1lb 5oz) new potatoes, scrubbed clean
6 spring onions, trimmed and finely sliced
3 tablespoons white wine vinegar
1 teaspoon smooth Dijon mustard
1 clove of garlic, finely chopped
3 tablespoons roughly chopped fresh parsley
9 tablespoons extra virgin olive oil
salt and freshly ground black pepper
340g (12oz) raw picante chorizo sausage, sliced
4 generous handfuls of rocket

1 Preheat the grill to its highest setting. Place the chillies and pepper quarters, skin-side-up, under the grill until they begin to blister and blacken. Turn the chillies regularly. Transfer to a covered bowl. Once cool, peel all the peppers and peel, de-stalk and deseed the chillies. Cut both into broad strips and place in a large bowl.

2 Drop the potatoes into a pan of boiling water. Cook for 15 minutes, or until tender; drain. Once cool, slice and mix with the onions. Whisk together the vinegar, mustard, garlic, parsley, 8 tablespoons of oil and seasoning. Divide between the peppers and potatoes.

3 Briskly fry the chorizo in the remaining tablespoon of oil until crisp and lightly coloured on both sides. Drain on kitchen paper and mix into the potato salad. Toss the rocket into the peppers, mix into the potatoes and serve warm or at room temperature.

marinades

All forms of chilli can be used in marinades, but the longer an ingredient is marinated, the hotter it is likely to taste. Sweet ingredients, such as honey or sugar, appear to lessen our perception of chilli heat, just as certain acidic ingredients, such as vinegar or citrus juice, seem to increase it. It is, however, essential to match your chilli to the cooking method. Dried chilli flakes and powders, for example, can easily burn and imbue a dish with a bitter taste, making fresh chillies more suited to recipes that sear fish or meat. There are exceptions, such as with 'blackened' Cajun dishes where paprika and cayenne are mixed with other spices to coat an ingredient that is then burnt in hot margarine.

lemon, paprika and honey grilled chicken

This simple sweet and sour marinade, with its delicate bitter-tasting olive oil, is transformed by the addition of smoked paprika, which adds a tantalizing complexity to the grilled meat.

serves 4

2 teaspoons runny honey
1 small clove of garlic, finely chopped
½ lemon, juiced
1 tablespoon extra virgin olive oil
½ teaspoon smoked paprika
salt and freshly ground black pepper
4 boneless chicken breasts, skinned

1 Whisk together the honey, garlic, lemon juice, olive oil and paprika in a medium-sized bowl. Season to taste.

2 Trim the chicken breasts of any excess fat or bloody areas. Remove the fillet and peel away its membrane. Take the first chicken breast and – once trimmed – place between 2 sheets of clingfilm. Using a rolling pin, gently flatten it into a thin escalope. Repeat the process with the remaining chicken breasts. Once flattened, mix with the fillets into the marinade, cover and chill for 20 minutes.

3 Preheat an oven-top grill-pan over a medium high heat. Grill the chicken for 4–5 minutes on each side. Serve hot, warm or cold.

kashmiri lamb curry

Toasted dried chilli works particularly well when combined with other spices. The flavours merge together to create a luscious aromatic depth, while the heat of the chilli helps to prevent the palate being swamped by the myriad different tastes and aromas.

serves 6

3 dried Kashmiri chillies
2 teaspoons fennel seeds
2 teaspoons coriander seeds
½ teaspoon black peppercorns
6 green cardamoms
1 kg (2lb 3oz) lamb leg, trimmed and diced
5 tablespoons sunflower oil
a pinch of saffron threads
3 onions, finely sliced
2 cloves of garlic, finely diced
½ teaspoon finely chopped fresh ginger
1 teaspoon garam masala
140ml (¼ pint) double cream
salt
200g (7oz) natural Greek yoghurt

1 Set a small frying pan over a medium-low heat and add the chillies. Gently roast, turning regularly, until lightly coloured and soft. Transfer to a spice grinder (mine is an old coffee grinder). Briefly grind to break up the chillies. Meanwhile, gently roast the fennel and coriander seeds, black peppercorns and whole cardamom pods until they smell fantastic. Tip into the grinder and whizz with the chillies until they form a fine powder. Mix into the lean diced lamb with 1 tablespoon of oil. Cover and chill for 3–6 hours.

2 Put the saffron in a bowl with about 300ml (11fl oz) of warm water and leave to infuse. Pour the remaining oil into a saucepan and gently fry the onions, garlic and ginger for about 10 minutes, or until the onions are soft and golden. Mix in the garam masala, fry for 5 minutes, then increase the heat, add the spicy lamb and stir-fry until it is well coloured. Add the saffron water, cream and salt to taste. Cover and simmer for about 75–90 minutes, or until the lamb is tender. Remove from the heat, stir in the yoghurt and serve.

sauces

One of the best ways to add heat to a dish is via the sauce. It allows the cook to construct an exciting dish that can also counteract the effects of capsaicin through its creamy texture or sweet taste. There are many different kinds of chilli sauces ranging from refreshing fruit salsas to intensely rich cooked tomato sauces.

avocado salad with roasted red onion and spiced pepper sauce

This gorgeous dish combines all five tastes with an unctuous sweet and sour sauce, whose heat takes the eater by surprise. You can use any medium-hot red chilli. The onions can be eaten warm or at room temperature.

serves 4

1 red pepper, quartered and seeded
1 fresh red chilli (see above)
½ lime, juiced
2 tablespoons crème fraîche
salt and freshly ground black pepper
4 medium red onions, halved
10 tablespoons extra virgin olive oil
200g (7oz) smoked back bacon, diced
2 tablespoons white wine vinegar
2 ripe avocados
4–5 large handfuls of mixed bitter salad leaves

1 Preheat the oven to 180°C (350°F) gas mark 4. Turn the grill to its highest setting and grill the pepper quarters, skin-side-up, and the chilli. Grill until their skins begin to blister, turning the chilli so it is evenly cooked. Remove and put in a covered bowl.

2 Once cool, peel the peppers and place in a food processor with the lime juice. Peel the chilli, then pull away its stalk and remove the seeds. As chillies can vary in heat, start by adding a quarter or less to the peppers. Process to a purée and taste, adding more chilli if you wish. Transfer to a bowl and mix in the crème fraîche. Season to taste and set aside.

3 Put the onions in the baking tray. Toss in 2 tablespoons of oil, season, and bake in the preheated oven for 50 minutes until they are soft and lightly caramelized. Fry the bacon in 2 tablespoons of oil until crisp; drain on kitchen paper.

4 Whisk together the vinegar and 6 tablespoons of oil. Season to taste. Halve, stone and peel the avocados, then cut into long slices. Place these in a large mixing bowl and coat in half the dressing. Add the bacon, salad leaves and remaining vinaigrette. Mix, then divide between 4 plates in airy piles. Slip in the onion and drizzle with the pepper sauce. Serve immediately.

chilli garlic spaghetti

A classic example of a bitter-sweet, savoury chilli dish that enables you to experiment with the different tastes. Try it without salt initially, then add some, followed by some salty, umami-tasting Parmesan, before finally adding a squeeze of sour lemon. If feeling truly experimental, measure the effect of the chilli by making the recipe with and without it. Amazingly, the slippery shape of the spaghetti and its sweet taste as you bite into it is highlighted by the chilli's presence.

serves 2

170g (6oz) spaghetti
6 tablespoons extra virgin olive oil
2 cloves of garlic, finely diced
1 teaspoon chilli flakes
a large handful of fresh parsley, finely chopped
freshly grated Parmesan cheese and lemon wedges, optional

1 Drop the spaghetti into a saucepan of boiling, salted water. Cook the pasta until *al dente*, according to the packet instructions.

2 Shortly before the spaghetti is ready, measure the olive oil into a small frying pan. Add the garlic and place over a low heat so that the garlic infuses rather than cooks in the warm (not hot) oil. As soon as the spaghetti is *al dente*, briefly drain into a colander and return to its saucepan. Immediately increase the heat under the frying pan, add the chilli flakes and fry briskly for a couple of minutes. Take care not to burn the garlic or the chilli, otherwise they will taste bitter. Add the parsley and mix into the spaghetti. Add more oil, if necessary.

3 Serve with freshly grated Parmesan and lemon wedges, if wished.

lobster with papaya and lime salsa

There are many permutations of sweet and sour chilli sauces. Fruit salsas, in particular, benefit from a chilli that echoes their flavour, as this creates a more subtle tasting sauce.

serves 4

1 papaya
1 lime, juiced, plus 2 extra limes
3 tablespoons finely chopped fresh coriander
a pinch of finely diced, seeded habañero chilli
salt and freshly ground black pepper
4 small boiled lobsters
4 handfuls of mixed salad leaves
2 tablespoons very good extra virgin olive oil

1 Peel the papaya with a sharp knife. Cut the fruit in half, scrape out its seeds and cut into medium-fine dice. Put in a bowl with the lime juice and coriander. Add the pinch of finely chopped chilli to the salsa, then season to taste. Add more chilli, lime or seasoning as you wish.

2 Shell the lobsters, removing all their meat. Cut each torso in half lengthways. When you are ready to serve, plate each lobster, then quickly toss the salad leaves in the olive oil and season to taste. Divide the leaves between the 4 plates, before adding a spoonful of relish and a lime half to each plate. Serve immediately.

spiced duck breast with tamarind sauce

Another type of spicy sweet-sour sauce, which perfectly complements the rich umami taste of the duck.

serves 4

115g (4oz) tamarind pulp (with seeds)
1 tablespoon caster sugar
2 teaspoons salt
1 teaspoon garam masala
¼–½ teaspoon chilli powder or to taste
30g (1oz) sultanas
4 boneless duck breasts
½ teaspoon five-spice powder

1 To make the sauce, place the tamarind and 200ml (7fl oz) warm water in a bowl. Leave for 15 minutes, then gently rub the tamarind, separating the pulp from the stones. Strain through a coarse sieve and discard the fibres and stones. Mix in the sugar, 1 teaspoon of salt, garam masala, chilli powder to taste and sultanas. Simmer gently for 8 minutes, then remove from heat.

2 Trim the duck breasts of sinews and score their skin into diamonds. Mix 1 teaspoon of salt with the five-spice powder and rub into the duck breasts.

3 Place the duck breasts, skin-side-down, in a frying pan over a low heat. As soon as the fat in the skin begins to melt, increase the heat to medium and fry for about 5 minutes. Flip them over and fry until cooked; the duck will be pink inside after a further 5–6 minutes. If you want it cooked more, return it to the oven for a couple of minutes. Reheat the sauce and serve.

savoury dishes

Adding chilli to a savoury dish is like throwing in the magician's powder, as with a sudden explosive puff it brings the careful balance of taste and texture to life. As the mouth tingles with the heat, you become acutely aware of every aroma, taste and texture while you munch. It all tastes so exciting that, even when a dish is too hot, one feels compelled to take one bite after another! Of course, the art of a good cook is to handle such culinary dynamite with care. A hint of cayenne pepper in an egg sandwich or a drop of Tabasco in a prawn and avocado mayonnaise salad will be enough to transform them into the most delectable of dishes.

spiced chicken with chickpeas

Paprika is inextricably linked with goulash – so here is an unorthodox approach to the classic combination of paprika, tomatoes and soured cream. The paprika's mild, sweet heat excites the palate and enhances the sweet, sour and umami taste of the soured cream and tomatoes, making it superb.

serves 3

2 large boneless chicken breasts, skinned
1 tablespoon plain flour
salt and freshly ground black pepper
3 tablespoons extra virgin olive oil
1 small onion, finely diced
1 clove of garlic, finely diced
¼ teaspoon cumin seeds
1 teaspoon smoked paprika
370g (13oz) fresh tomatoes
410g can chickpeas, drained and rinsed
70ml (2.5fl oz) soured cream

1 Trim the chicken breasts of any fat and cut into easy-to-eat chunks. Mix the flour with some salt and freshly ground black pepper in a small bowl.

2 Heat the oil in a sauté pan. Toss the diced chicken in the seasoned flour, shake off the excess and add in a single layer to the pan. Fry briskly until well-coloured on all sides, then remove the chicken and reduce the heat before adding the onion and garlic to the pan, taking care to loosen any crusty chicken bits. Gently sauté for 4 minutes. Once the onion is soft, stir in the cumin seeds and paprika and cook for 2–3 minutes.

3 To peel the tomatoes, cut a cross in the base of each and cover with boiling water for a minute or two. Then drain, peel and roughly chop the tomatoes before mixing them into the spiced onions. Fry briskly, stirring regularly, until they form a thick purée, then mix in the chicken, chickpeas and 140ml (¼ pint) water. Season to taste and simmer gently for 10 minutes, or until the chicken is just cooked. Stir in the soured cream and reheat, but avoid boiling or the cream will split. Serve with a saffron rice (see p.200) for a sophisticated bitter-sweet twist.

chilli

blackened swordfish with pineapple salsa

Combining two types of chillies can enhance the flavour of both, as can be discovered in this recipe. The fish is coated and fried in a bitter aromatic spice mixture, which is sweetened by the predominance of paprika. It is then served with a sweet-sour pineapple salsa that has been infused with a fresh chilli. The result is an explosion of taste and flavour in the mouth and plates wiped clean. I have included this recipe here, rather than in the sauce section, as the dish only really works when fish and salsa are combined together.

serves 6

pineapple salsa

2 tablespoons light muscovado sugar
1 tablespoon white wine vinegar
100ml (3.5fl oz) sake
a pinch of saffron threads
1 jalapeño chilli, partially split
1 large ripe pineapple

blackened swordfish

5 tablespoons sweet paprika
1 tablespoon dried garlic granules
1 tablespoon dried onion powder
1½ teaspoons cayenne pepper
1½ teaspoons dried oregano
1½ teaspoons dried thyme
salt and freshly ground black pepper
6 skinned swordfish steaks
6 tablespoons olive oil
6 large sprigs of fresh flat-leaf parsley or coriander for garnish

1 Place the sugar, vinegar, sake, saffron and chilli in a small non-corrosive saucepan. Set over a low heat and stir until the sugar has dissolved. Cut away the pineapple skin, removing its eyes as you do so. Slice and core before cutting into medium-to-small dice. Add to the hot sake and leave to cool.

2 Mix together the paprika, dried garlic, onion powder, cayenne pepper, oregano and thyme in a bowl. Season well. If you can't find any dried onion powder, just add another tablespoon of dried garlic powder instead.

3 Preheat an oven-top grill-pan over a medium-high heat. Rub the swordfish steaks in half the olive oil, then lightly coat in the spice mixture. Once it has soaked in, lightly drizzle with the remaining olive oil, then grill the fish for 3 minutes on each side, so that the spices darken but don't burn as the fish cooks. At the same time, gently reheat the pineapple salsa until it is piping hot. As you plate the swordfish, partially cover with a spoonful or two of the hot salsa with its spicy juice, and garnish with a large sprig of flat-leaf parsley or coriander. If you like an extra spicy salsa, you can finely dice some of the infused jalapeño chillies as a garnish.

spicy stir-fried purple-sprouting broccoli

The heat of dried cayenne chilli flakes pricks the palate and enlivens the bitter-sweet nature of stir-fried

serves 2

200g (7oz) purple-sprouting broccoli, trimmed
2 tablespoons sunflower oil
1 clove of garlic, cut into fine strips
4 thin rounds of fresh ginger, cut into fine strips
a pinch of chilli flakes
salt

1 Cut the thicker broccoli stems at an angle to make attractive, fast-cooking slices. Set aside. Preheat a frying pan or a wok. Add the oil and once it is hot, add the garlic, ginger and chilli flakes. Stir-fry for a second and, as soon as they sizzle, add the broccoli and continue to stir-fry briskly until it turns bright green and is just cooked. Season with salt and serve immediately.

stir-fried chilli pork balls

The clean flavour of fresh Thai chillies reduces the potentially rank, bloody taste of meat by enhancing its sweeter elements – as do ginger and spring onions. It may seem odd to combine pork with prawns, but I love this subtle-flavoured stir-fry; it's delicious with steamed rice.

serves 4

225g (8oz) raw shelled tiger prawns
2 Thai chillies, or to taste, finely chopped
1 bunch of spring onions, finely sliced
1 teaspoon finely chopped fresh ginger
finely grated zest of 2 limes
450g (1lb) minced pork
5 tablespoons soy sauce
3 tablespoons sake
2 cloves of garlic, finely chopped
5 tablespoons sunflower oil
170g (6oz) shiitake mushrooms
1 teaspoon caster sugar
2 teaspoons cornflour
200g (7oz) pak choi, roughly sliced

1 Clean the prawns by cutting a small incision along the length of their back and removing the dark digestive cord. Rinse, pat dry and roughly chop. Set aside in a bowl. Put the chillies, onions, ginger, lime zest, pork, 2 tablespoons of soy sauce, 1 tablespoon of sake and half the garlic in a processor. Process in short bursts, so the mince is finer but does not form a paste. Beat into the prawns and shape about 44 walnut-sized balls.

2 Heat a tablespoon of oil in a large frying pan. As soon as it is hot, gently fry half the pork balls for about 8 minutes, or until cooked. Remove and repeat the process with the second batch.

3 Rip the mushrooms into large pieces, discarding their stems. Mix the remaining soy sauce and sake with the sugar, cornflour and 8 tablespoons of water. Set a wok or frying pan over a high heat, add 3 tablespoons of oil and, when very hot, add remaining garlic, mushrooms and pork balls. Stir-fry briskly for 2 minutes, then add the pak choi. After seconds, add the sauce ingredients. Boil until this thickens slightly and serve.

puddings and cakes

My love of chillies has led me to experiment with them in puddings. I discovered that they have a natural affinity to some puddings, in particular chocolate and sweet and sour fruit dishes. The heat should be used like a spice, so that it gently tingles in the mouth as you eat. This subtlety will be lost if such puddings are served after a spicy meal. The key is to choose a chilli that will echo the flavours you want to create in your pudding – for example, a fruit salad is best when seasoned with a 'fruity' flavoured chilli such as a habañero, whereas a bitter gooey chocolate pudding needs the punchy aroma of a dried chilli such as a Kashmiri or Pasilla chilli.

spiced tropical fruit salad

This recipe is the perfect way to introduce friends to the charms of chilli-spiced puddings. It tastes fantastic – no doubt due to the perfect combination of sweet and sour, mixed with glorious fruity flavours, which the habañero picks up. The vanilla, incidentally, enhances the sweetness, which in turn lessens the heat of the chilli.

serves 4–6

1 lemon
115g (4oz) caster sugar
1 habañero chilli
1 vanilla pod
5 black peppercorns
2 star anise
1 small pineapple
1 ripe mango
8 lychees
8 physalis
2 bananas
1 granadilla

1 Finely pare 3–4 strips of peel from the lemon, then put this in a small non-corrosive saucepan with the sugar, chilli, vanilla pod, peppercorns, star anise and about 300ml (11fl oz) water. Set over a medium heat, stirring occasionally until the sugar has dissolved, then simmer gently for 10 minutes. Remove from the heat and add the juice of the lemon.

2 Meanwhile, peel the pineapple, remove its eyes, cut into chunks and place in an attractive bowl. Peel the mango and cut its flesh away from the stone in 4 segments. Cut each segment into easy-to-eat slices and add to the pineapple. Peel and stone the lychees and add to the fruit. Pull the physalis out of its paper husk and rinse before cutting in half. Peel and slice the bananas and add these, with the physalis, to the fruit salad. Immediately add the warm spiced syrup and mix thoroughly.

3 Finally, cut the granadilla in half and scoop out its gelatinous seeds. Mix into the fruit salad and set aside. The longer the spices are left in the salad, the more spicy it will become. I always leave them in, as they look so beautiful. This is not a dish to serve with cream.

sticky orange chilli vodka cake

Infusing Kashmiri chillies into a sticky orange and almond cake might seem odd, but they add an intriguing, indefinable tingle as one eats, which highlights the sweet, sour and mildly bitter nature of the cake. Definitely an adult cake, especially as the vodka adds a further kick.

serves 6

170g (6oz) softened butter, plus extra
for greasing
170g (6oz) caster sugar
1½ oranges
3 large eggs, separated
85g (3oz) self-raising flour, sifted
85ml (3fl oz) dessert wine
85g (3oz) ground almonds
1 lemon
30g (1oz) granulated sugar
2 dried Kashmiri chillies
3 tablespoons vodka

1 Preheat the oven to 170°C (325°F) gas mark 3. Butter a 20cm (8-inch) spring-form cake tin. Beat the butter and caster sugar until pale and fluffy. Finely grate the zest of 1 orange, add to the sweetened butter, then gradually beat in the egg yolks, followed by 2 tablespoons of flour and the dessert wine. Lightly fold in half the almonds, followed by half the remaining flour. Next fold in the remaining almonds and the last of the flour.

2 Immediately whisk the egg whites in a clean, dry bowl until they form firm peaks. Quickly fold them into the cake mix, then spoon the mixture into the cake tin and place in the centre of the oven. Bake for 50 minutes, or until a skewer comes out clean. Turn out and place on a cooling rack over a deep-rimmed plate.

3 While the cake is baking, use a potato peeler to finely pare the lemon and remaining ½ orange. Place all the peel, the granulated sugar, dried chillies and 100ml (3.5fl oz) of water in a small non-corrosive saucepan. Dissolve the sugar over a low heat, then simmer gently for 10 minutes. Cover, remove from the heat and leave to infuse. Meanwhile, squeeze the juice from the 1½ oranges and ½ the lemon.

4 As soon as the cake is turned out of its tin, return the syrup to the heat and bring up to the boil. Add the fruit juice and vodka and strain into a jug. Prick the warm cake with a fork and drip-feed the syrup into the cake in small batches. Make sure it is evenly fed and use all the syrup – it's surprising how much a cake will absorb. Serve once cold.

chilli chocolate fondants

The heat of the chilli subtley underlines the spicy, bitter-sweet nature of this gooey chocolate pudding. Pasilla chillies have a fruity, wine-like taste that is perfect for this dish. Once cooked, the fondants should release a runny, mousse-like chocolate sauce, so timing is everything when cooking.

serves 8

115g (4oz) butter, plus extra for greasing
20g (¾oz) plain flour, plus extra for dusting
225g (8oz) dark chocolate, roughly chopped
2–3 teaspoons toasted, ground dried Pasilla or Kashmiri chillies (see p.166 for method)
115g (4oz) caster sugar
4 medium eggs, plus 1 medium yolk
icing sugar for dusting

1 Liberally butter 8 x 150ml (5½fl oz) metal pudding basins up to the rim. Put a circle of buttered greaseproof paper in the bottom of each basin and lightly dust with flour. Freeze for 30 minutes. Melt the chocolate and butter in a bowl over a bowl of just boiled water (you may need to replace the water once); stir occasionally. Once melted and well amalgamated, remove from heat.

2 Mix the chilli, sugar, eggs and egg yolk in a large bowl. Using an electric whisk, beat the egg mixture for a good 5 minutes, until thick and pale. Sift the flour over the beaten eggs and, using a metal spoon, lightly fold it in. Fold in the chocolate. Immediately spoon into the 8 buttered containers and chill for at least 30 minutes. Preheat the oven to 200°C (400°F) gas mark 6. Bake the fondants for 12–14 minutes, until still wobbly but lightly risen with a slight crust. Remove and rest for 2 minutes. Gently run a knife around their edges before inverting on to plates. When ready to serve, remove the basins, dust with icing sugar and serve immediately.

grape sorbet

The delicate prickly heat of chilli melts in the mouth in this refreshing grape and lime sorbet. The combination of ice and heat is very exciting and cleanses the palate in a delicious way.

serves 6

1 kg (2lb 3oz) flavoursome grapes, muscat for instance, stalked
1–2 habañero chillies (1 gives a mild prickle)
115g (4oz) caster sugar
1 lime, juiced
3 tablespoons good dessert wine

1 Put grapes in a non-corrosive pan with chillies, sugar and 3 tablespoons water over a low heat. Simmer for 10 minutes, stirring occasionally, until sugar dissolves and grapes start to collapse. Crush grapes and simmer for 5 minutes. Tip into a strainer over a bowl, add chillies to the bowl and leave to drip. Once cold, add lime and dessert wine. Cover and chill. Remove chilli and churn in an ice cream machine. Transfer to freezer for 2 hours.

preserves

Since preserves are frequently served as an intense, stimulating flavouring to other dishes, chillies have always been part of the battery of commonly used flavourings. A few dried chillies or a pinch of cayenne pepper have been added to chutneys, pickles, vinegars and oils for centuries. In recent years, however, cooks have also begun to add them to fruit jellies, finding their heat gives a subtle bite when combined with roast meat, fowl or game.

spiced plum jelly

I developed this sweet-sour recipe to accompany grilled duck, but it is equally good eaten with cold ham, melted into a game sauce or in a sweet plum pie.

makes about 1.4kg (3lb)

1kg (2lb 3oz) plums, quartered and stoned
1 star anise
1 fresh chilli of your choice
½ stick cinnamon
approx 1kg (2lb 3oz) sugar with pectin

1 Place the plums in a saucepan with the spices and 400ml (14fl oz) of water. Cover and bring up to the boil, then simmer gently until the fruit has disintegrated into a soft mush.

2 Tip into a jelly bag and leave to drip over a bowl for a minimum of 12 hours. Discard the pulp.

3 Measure the resulting juice. Allow 450g (1lb) of sugar with pectin for every 450ml (16fl oz) of plum juice. Put the juice and sugar in a jam pan and set over a low heat. Stir occasionally until the sugar has melted, then increase the heat and boil rapidly for a minute, or until setting point – 105°C (221°F) – has been reached. Skim off any scum and pour into warm jam jars that you have sterilized (by washing in soapy water, rinsing and drying in a very low oven). Cover and label. Store in a cool, dark place.

chilli notes

A quick way to add fiery heat to stir-fries, noodles, pasta sauces and stews is to add a dash of home-made Chinese red pepper oil. Measure 5 tablespoons of sunflower or peanut oil into a small saucepan and heat until hot but not smoking. Remove from the heat and wait for 30 seconds, then stir in 4 teaspoons of chilli powder. If the oil is too hot the chilli will scorch, making the oil taste unpleasantly bitter. Leave to infuse until cold before straining through a kitchen paper towels. Store in a sterilized jar, but use within a couple of weeks or the oil will taste stale.

Ready-made chilli sauces are invaluable as a source of spicy heat that can be added by the eater rather than by the cook. Tabasco or Chinese chilli sauce, for example, will add an instant fiery, fruity heat to any dish, but especially to umami-rich foods such as seared scallops, prawns or shiitake mushrooms.

A sprinkling of cayenne pepper will lighten the rich salty-sweet taste of buttery dishes such as creamy scrambled eggs, potted shrimp or smoked trout paté. Like a squeeze of lemon juice, it enlivens the appetite and revitalizes potentially monotonous dishes.

A fresh chilli lime butter is a refreshing way to spice up barbecued fish, meat and vegetables, especially tuna, beef and corn on the cob. Make it to taste by beating together 55g (2oz) softened unsalted butter with finely chopped (seeded) green or red chilli, the zest of a finely grated lime and 2 tablespoons of finely chopped fresh coriander. Then season to taste with lime juice, salt and freshly ground black pepper. Remember that the heat of the chilli will increase slightly as it sits in the butter, so be cautious – you can always add more. Roll into a smooth sausage in wet greaseproof paper. Chill and cut as needed.

Beautiful pickled green chillies are a brilliant way of adding mild heat to dishes that you wish to keep relatively unspiced. Buy from shops and serve as a garnish or an accompaniment and allow your guests to help themselves. They're wonderful eaten with hummus and crudités, for example, or with stuffed tortillas.

Some chilli addicts have taken to mixing roughly ground dried chillies into their sea salt to use as a seasoning on their food. Choose your favourite type of dried chilli, remove and discard its seeds, and lightly roast for a couple of minutes in a dry pan over a low heat. Allow to cool, then roughly grind the chillies into flakes and mix, according to your taste, with coarse sea salt. Take care when handling, as the chilli could still burn your hands when you crush the salt between your fingers. Alternatively, buy some ready-mixed chilli salt.

Finely sliced fresh chilli will perk up a simple soy-honey marinade for barbecued meat. To prepare the marinade, mix together 1 tablespoon of honey, 2 tablespoons of soy sauce, 1 tablespoon of lemon juice and 3 tablespoons of olive oil. Add some freshly sliced chilli to taste, along with a clove of finely chopped garlic and some freshly chopped coriander. Marinate the meat for 20–30 minutes and then grill it on the barbecue as normal.

Spicy pickles, chutneys and jellies are another subtle way of adding heat to a meal. Chilli suits them all, from the bitter-salty-sour Indian lime pickle to the heavily spiced gooseberry chutney and the sweet and sour pot of blackberry jelly. Most forms of fresh or dried chillies lend themselves to preserves, but it is important to remember that, if chilli is left in the pickle or chutney, its heat will continue to increase as the pickle or chutney matures.

flavours

It is impossible to imagine cooking without spices, herbs and fragrant distillations. I gain intense pleasure from adding a drop of this or a hint of that when cooking. It's like casting a spell with potions to bring out the subtle underlying flavours of a dish. Such aromas are omnipresent in food, from a sweet-smelling peach to a ripe cheese. Unlike the soluble compounds that are detected by the taste cells in the mouth (oral cavity), flavour (aroma) is airborne and is detected by the olfactory cells in the roof of the nasal cavity. In other words, as you eat, your breath passes into your nose imbued with the scent of your food. Naturally, this alters your perception of how it tastes, as anyone with a cold can vouchsafe.

Just as with taste, so everyone has different sensitivities to flavour. According to Peter Barham in his book *The Science of Cooking*, about a third of the population cannot smell the pungent aroma of woodland truffles and therefore cannot 'taste' them. Clearly a financial saving, if a physical loss. However, such thoughts should not influence cooks, who must always rely on their own sensitivities when flavouring food. Instead, it is more helpful to consider how different 'flavourings' can enhance certain tastes. And by 'flavourings', I mean spices, herbs and distilled flower waters, all of which are partly detected by their aroma and are usually added in small quantities.

Traditionally, certain herbs and spices are considered 'sweet'. This is because their aroma enhances the sweetness of a dish; thus, bay leaves give the illusion of imbuing a stock with sweetness, just as rosemary makes roast potatoes taste sweeter and fennel seeds make figs seem more sugary. Marjoram, mint, cinnamon and cloves all have a similar effect, regardless of whether they are added to a sweet or a savoury dish. Other flavourings can be used to emphasize bitterness or sourness. Mustard seeds, cumin and juniper berries, for example, underline any inherent bitterness, while dried pomegranate seeds, powdered green mango (amchoor powder) and lime leaves enhance sourness. I am not aware of any flavourings that emphasis saltiness. As to umami, since it tends to intensify our perception of sweetness, many 'sweet' flavourings work well with it.

The best way to develop a subtle use of flavouring is to sniff or nibble your chosen flavouring raw, then mentally match it with different tastes. When cooking, analyze how it affects the other ingredients and shape your recipes accordingly. It is easy to imagine how a spice such as cinnamon will taste in an apple pie or how distilled rose water will taste in a raspberry jelly. Fresh herbs, such as chervil, however, change their flavour slightly when cooked. The solution is to test eat some that have been roughly chopped and fried in a little beaten unseasoned egg. Once tasted, never forgotten.

parsley

If there is one ingredient that adjusts and balances the flavour of European and Mediterranean cooking, it is parsley *(Petroselinum crispum)*. Its vibrant, mildly bitter leaves add a refreshing mineral-like flavour to food by counterbalancing the cloying nature of sweet, salty and umami tastes, and balancing sour tastes. Caramelized onion soup, for example, tastes fresher if parsley is added just before serving, just as a citrus marinade is softened slightly by its addition. Parsley even emphasizes the sweetness in other bitter ingredients such as olives, chicory or salsify.

Parsley stems have the most flavour and are therefore best added to slow-cooking stocks, stews, soups and sauces. Its leaves should always be well washed to remove any grit before being dried and used. For maximum flavour, add at the last minute to a dish, whether it's an omelette, sautéed mushrooms or marinated grilled courgettes.

tabbouleh

In this recipe, parsley is used in such quantities that it is both a flavouring and a taste. Here, its mildly bitter taste is combined with similarly mildly bitter olive oil and sour lemon juice to enhance the sweetness of the bulgur wheat, making an appetizing and refreshing dish.

serves 4

115g (4oz) bulgur wheat
200g (7oz) tomatoes, peeled and quartered
115g (4oz) flat-leaf parsley, leaves and stems finely chopped
6 spring onions, finely sliced
½ ridge cucumber, finely diced
1 lemon, juiced
140ml (¼ pint) extra virgin olive oil
salt and freshly ground black pepper
2 little gem lettuces or 8 warm pitta bread

1 Pour some boiling water over the bulgur wheat and leave to soak for 15 minutes. Drain in a sieve, rinse under the cold tap and squeeze dry. Set aside.

2 De-seed and dice the tomatoes, saving the seeds and juice. Strain the latter into a mixing bowl. Add the diced tomato flesh and the prepared bulgur wheat. Leave while you prepare the remaining ingredients.

3 Mix the parsley stems with the spring onions and cucumber. Add to the tomato mixture, mix in the lemon juice and olive oil and season to taste. Serve with little gem lettuce leaves or pitta bread.

fresh ginger

Fresh ginger (Zingiber officinale) is a key ingredient in Chinese and Japanese cooking, where it is used to create delicious food by the seemingly artless effect of enhancing the good and masking the bad in each ingredient. Its intense aroma helps suppress offensive flavours in meat, poultry and seafood. In other words it dispels the bloody, bitter taste in meat and the oily, fishy aroma in seafood, which makes it a useful component in marinades and broths. Ginger's flavour is both hot and refreshing. It underlines sour citrus notes in recipes and imbues salty, umami, sour and sweet dishes with a delicate freshness. However, the natural warmth of ginger will predominate if added to a very sweet or bitter dish such as ginger poached pears or chocolate ginger cake.

Always choose plump, smooth-looking fresh ginger rhizomes for maximum juiciness. Dried ginger root and powdered ginger have different effects on taste, emphasizing a warm sweetness rather than a stimulating freshness.

ginger-soy dipping sauce with tempura

Ginger is infused into this addictive salty-umami dipping sauce to help to bring out the innate sweetness of the deep-fried prawns and bitter-sweet asparagus.

serves 4

dipping sauce
4 tablespoons Kikkoman soy sauce
4 tablespoons mirin
4 tablespoons sake
1 tablespoon finely chopped fresh ginger

tempura
20 asparagus tips
12 raw tiger prawns
1 egg yolk
225ml (8fl oz) iced water
115g (4oz) plain flour, sifted, plus extra for dipping

1 Put the soy sauce, mirin, sake and ginger in a small pan. Simmer gently for 5 minutes. Remove from the heat and mix in 4 tablespoons of warm water. Leave to cool. Wash and pat dry the asparagus. Twist off the prawns' heads and remove the shells, apart from the tail tip. Run a knife down the back of each prawn and pull away the black digestive cord; rinse and pat dry. The prawns and asparagus must be dry before being floured and battered.

2 Heat the oil to 170°C (325°F). Put the egg yolk in a bowl and add the iced water. Using a chopstick, roughly mix with 1 or 2 strokes. Sift in the flour and barely mix, so the batter is still lumpy. When ready, toss the asparagus in the extra flour before dipping it into the batter, then drop into the oil. Fry the asparagus in batches for about 3 minutes, turning once; the batter should barely colour. Drain and leave on kitchen paper.

3 Increase the oil temperature to 180°C (350°F). Repeat the process with the prawns. They too will take about 3 minutes. Arrange the prawns and asparagus on plates with the sauce in little bowls. Serve immediately.

black pepper

Even when a kitchen is bare of spices, you will usually find a small pot of black pepper hidden in the cupboard. Admittedly, it might be ready-ground and have lost most of its fragrance, but it will still contain a hint of piperine, the bitter alkaloid that stimulates the mouth to water and aids digestion. It is this, combined with a volatile oil, that gives pepper its mouth-tingling pungency. Its complex, almost sweet aroma, however, is best released by freshly grinding some black peppercorns into a dish at the end of cooking. Like chilli, it will enhance your perception of all five tastes regardless of whether it is sprinkled on to a sweet slice of melon or a sour scoop of fresh goat's cheese.

Black pepper is the dried, unripe berries of *Piper nigrum*, an Indian climbing vine. White pepper is partially fermented, skinned, dried, ripe berries of the same vine. The latter lacks the aroma of the black pepper and is normally used for aesthetic reasons rather than flavour, by cooks fearful of the black granules being misconstrued as specks of dirt. Pepper will last indefinitely if stored in a cool, dark, airtight container. Buy the best quality, free from stalk and dust.

peppered venison steak

Any fish or meat lightly coated with crushed peppercorns will taste surprisingly sweet and fresh. Here, the pepper also plays with the sweet-sour-umami sauce, making it even more scrumptious.

serves 4

1 heaped tablespoon whole black peppercorns
20g (¾oz) plain flour
a pinch salt
3 tablespoons olive oil
6 trimmed venison steaks, each about 140g (5oz)
2 tablespoons brandy
1 clove of garlic, finely chopped
200ml (7fl oz) chicken stock (see p.202)
140ml (¼ pint) good red wine
4 tablespoons port
2 finely pared strips of lemon peel
1 tablespoon redcurrant jelly
30g (1oz) butter

1 Preheat the oven to its lowest setting. Roughly crush the peppercorns and mix into the flour with the salt.

2 Heat the olive oil in a large frying pan over a medium heat. Lightly coat the venison steaks with the peppercorn mixture and fry briskly, colouring both sides. Once medium-rare, pour the brandy over and set alight, standing well back. Allow the alcohol to burn off, then transfer the steaks to the warm oven.

3 Add the garlic to the frying pan and sauté for a few seconds, then stir in the stock, red wine, port and lemon peel. Boil vigorously, scraping the pan as you do so, until the sauce has reduced slightly and is well flavoured. Whisk in the redcurrant jelly, adjust the seasoning to taste and remove the lemon peel. Take off the heat, whisk in the butter and return the steaks to the sauce. Serve immediately.

cinnamon

Cinnamon was once regarded as one of the 'sweet' spices. It imbues all that it flavours with a delicate warmth and satisfying complex sweetness, regardless of whether the dish is a savoury lamb tagine or a sticky bun. Cinnamon deepens the sweet-umami nature of duck, lamb or beef and counteracts the sourness of wine or fruit. Imagine mulled wine, claret jelly or apple strudel without a hint of cinnamon. It heightens the sweet complexity of a cake, custard or ice-cream and softens the bitterness of chocolate, treacle and caramel by implying an underlying sweetness. It is also a prime constituent in curry powders, balancing the bitterness of turmeric and softening the heat of chilli.

Cinnamon's fragile quills are planed from the inner bark of a camphor laurel *(Cinnamomum zelyanicum)* indigenous to Sri Lanka, and should not be confused with the coarser-looking rolled quills of cassia, which has a more pungent flavour. Cinnamon quickly loses its aroma once ground and should always be stored in a cool, dark place.

grilled cinnamon apple rings

The cinnamon enhances the sweet, aromatic taste of these grilled apples.

serves 4

4 dessert apples, such as Cox or Braeburn
3 tablespoons lemon juice
1 tablespoon icing sugar
½ teaspoon ground cinnamon
55g (2oz) butter, melted

1 Preheat an oven-top grill-pan over a medium-high heat. Core and peel the apples, cutting them into 5mm (¼-inch) thick rounds and mixing them in lemon juice as you go. Sift together the icing sugar and cinnamon.

2 Toss the apple rings in the melted butter and arrange half in a single layer on the grill-pan. Cook for about 2 minutes, or until they are flecked gold, then turn over and grill for a further 3 minutes. Quickly dust with the cinnamon icing sugar and turn once again for a few seconds until the sugar caramelizes. Remove and keep warm while you repeat the process with the remaining apple rings.

3 Serve warm with clotted cream or crème fraîche.

cumin

The intriguing bitterness of cumin seeds is only activated once they are subjected to heat. Scatter a few pungent cumin seeds *(Cuminum cyminum)* into a dry pan and gently roast them over a low heat until the kitchen is filled with a tantalizing earthy fragrance. Their aromatic bitter scent will add an irresistible allure to sour, salty, umami and sweet dishes. Soured cream, tamarind water and lemon juice, for example, all taste sweeter with a last-minute seasoning of ground roasted cumin seeds. But take care not to burn them, otherwise they will impart an unpleasantly bitter taste.

Alternatively, they can be cooked unroasted as part of a dish. Cumin ground and rubbed raw into uncooked lamb or beef, for example, will deepen the umami taste when roasted with the meat, just as its whole seeds will intensify the sweetness of onions, peas, potatoes and pulses when sautéed in oil or butter. It is very good combined with other bitter ingredients such as aubergine, cauliflower or cucumber, as it highlights any natural sweetness by deepening their intrinsic bitterness. Cumin also has a natural affinity with the heat of chillies, regardless of whether it is in an Indian curry or South American spiced chilli.

raita

The alluring bitterness of roasted cumin seeds adds a complexity to the refreshing sour taste of salted yoghurt. This is delicious eaten with lightly spiced grilled meat, curried red kidney beans and dry vegetable curries such as green bean and potato, or cauliflower and potato.

serves 4

255g (9oz) natural Greek yoghurt, chilled
½ cucumber or 1 ridge of cucumber, peeled and roughly grated
salt and freshly ground black pepper
½ teaspoon cumin seeds

1 Place the yoghurt in a mixing bowl and whisk in enough cold water (you will need about 140ml (¼ pint) if your yoghurt is nice and thick) to make a creamy thick sauce. Mix in the cucumber and season to taste with salt and freshly ground black pepper. Pour into a serving bowl.

2 Place the cumin seeds in a small dry frying pan and set over a low heat. Shake the pan regularly to move the seeds and cook for about 3 minutes or until they darken slightly and release an amazing fragrance. Remove and grind them under a rolling pin or in a pestle and mortar until they form a fine powder. Sprinkle over the cucumber yoghurt and serve immediately.

cardamom

Break open the pale green pod of the cardamom plant *(Elettaria cardamomum)* and you will discover tiny, aromatic black and brown seeds whose zingy, camphor-like flavour adds an indefinable freshness to sweet foods, regardless of whether it is a savoury rice pilaff or a bitter-sweet cup of cardamom coffee. Thus, if you wish to lighten a sweet-tasting food, try infusing it with a little cardamom. It has a natural affinity with sautéed onion, cream, rice, butter, sugar and delicate-flavoured fruits such as pears or peaches. Curiously, cardamom has the reverse effect with mildly sour or bitter foods. It enhances the natural sweetness of oranges or lemons, just as it lessens the bitterness of coffee or chocolate.

Once ground, cardamom quickly releases its volatile oils, so always buy whole pods, rather than powdered seeds. It should not be confused with Indian black cardamom, a different spice entirely, which has an intense, slightly antiseptic aroma that demands strong flavours.

cardamom ice-cream

The cardamom lightens the intense sweetness of this ice-cream. Compare it with the sweet taste of the vanilla custard on page 201.

serves 4

10 green cardamom pods
425ml (¾ pint) double cream
6 egg yolks
85g (3oz) caster sugar

1 Lightly crush the cardamom pods and tip them, seeds and all, into a saucepan with the cream. Set over a low heat and scald by bringing up to just below boiling point. Remove from the heat, cover and leave to infuse for 30 minutes. Find two large bowls, one of which will sit inside the other. Fill the larger bowl with ice and rest the smaller one on it; set aside.

2 Whisk the egg yolks with the sugar until they are pale, then stir in the cardamom cream. Return to a clean pan and place over a low heat. Keep stirring with a wooden spoon for 10–20 minutes, until you have thick custard. Do not let the custard boil or leave it unattended. Pour into the bowl on the ice. Keep stirring until it is tepid, then strain into a clean container, cover and chill.

3 Once cold, process the custard in an ice-cream maker, according to the manufacturer's instructions. Alternatively, freeze it in a container, mixing it thoroughly with a fork every hour or so to ensure an even distribution of ice crystals – this will take a good 6 hours. If using the following day, allow the ice-cream to soften slightly in the fridge before serving.

mint

Every cook knows that mint *(Mentha spicata)* enhances the sweetness of boiled vegetables. Its aromatic oil is released when bruised and can be infused into everything from buttered new potatoes to a refreshing apple sorbet. It seems to amplify sweetness in food – for example, in carrots, peas and beetroot as well as shellfish, salmon and lamb. This aspect can be further intensified by combining mint with sweet-and-sour tasting ingredients, such as sugar and vinegar or honey and lime juice. Mint will add a sweet note to mildly bitter, sour or salty dishes, such as steamed spinach tossed with crème fraîche, grapefruit salad, or noodles with soy and honey dressing. There are many varieties of mint, including the intensely scented Moroccan mint (perfect for tea), apple mint, lemon mint, ginger mint and the hybrid, peppermint. The last is best used in tisanes as it is very strong. Avoid dried mint; it tends to have a musty flavour.

pakoras with mint chutney

An Indian take on mint sauce! Its sweet-sour nature enhances the delicate, sweet and bitter tastes of the vegetable fritters. It is also good with tandoori dishes (see p.28), meat kebabs and shellfish. Gram flour and sour-tasting anardana powder are available from specialist Indian shops.

serves 6

sunflower oil for deep-frying
1 medium onion
2 medium potatoes, peeled
255g (9oz) cauliflower
½ teaspoon each of salt, garam masala and chilli powder

batter

170g (6oz) gram flour
1 teaspoon each of garam masala and salt
½ teaspoon each of ground turmeric and chilli powder

mint chutney

40g (1½oz) fresh mint leaves, finely chopped
2 limes, juiced
½ small green chilli, seeded and finely chopped
6 spring onions, finely chopped
½ teaspoon each of salt and garam masala
2 teaspoons sugar
¾ teaspoon anardana powder (ground dried pomegranate seeds), optional

1 Heat the oil in a deep-fat fryer to 190°C (375°F). Cut the onion into thick rings, slice the potatoes into thick rounds and cut the cauliflower into medium-thick florets. Pat dry on kitchen paper and mix with the salt and spices.

2 Sift all the batter ingredients into a bowl and slowly beat in 200ml (7fl oz) of water until you have a smooth, thick batter. Dip the potato slices into it, making sure they are properly coated, then fry for 5–6 minutes, until the potato is just cooked and the batter is golden brown. Drain on kitchen paper and set aside to cool. Repeat the process with the cauliflower. Finally, add the onion rings. These will only need to cook for about 4 minutes each. Leave until cold.

3 Combine all the ingredients for the mint chutney. When ready to serve, reheat the oil to 190°C (375°F) and refry the potatoes and cauliflower for 2–3 minutes and the onions for 1 minute. Drain on kitchen paper and serve hot or warm with the chutney.

nutmeg

In the eighteenth century, 'civilized' people carried a small nutmeg grater about their person to ensure that they could grate its warm, lemony, fragrance into their punch or hot chocolate at a moment's notice. Its aroma quickly fades once grated, so even when cooking it is essential to add it at the last moment. Nutmeg's peppery warmth comes from myristicin, which in large quantities is a poisonous narcotic. In the small quantities used in cooking, nutmeg adds a sweet lightness to bitter greens, sweet milk dishes and umami tomato-based meat stews. It lightens creamy fish dishes, imbues all meat with a sweet freshness and adds a hint of lemon to spiced cakes. Sprinkled on to a rum punch (see p127) it teases the appetite into taking further sips.

Nutmeg *(Myristica fragrans)* is the speckled brown seed of the nutmeg tree. It is encased in a scarlet aril, which is sold as mace, once the two are separated and dried. It should be kept airtight in a cool, dark place.

tagliatelle with spinach sauce

Nutmeg, mixed with lemon zest adds a tantalizing freshness to the bitter-sweet combination of spinach, sautéed shallots and mascarpone.

serves 4

salt
400g (14oz) dried tagliatelle
450g (1lb) baby spinach leaves
3 tablespoons olive oil
4 shallots, halved and finely sliced
2 cloves of garlic, finely diced
a pinch of dried chilli flakes, optional
170g (6oz) mascarpone cheese
finely grated peel of 2 lemons
freshly ground black pepper
generous pinch of freshly grated nutmeg
8 tablespoons freshly grated Parmesan cheese,
plus extra to serve

1 Bring 2 large pans of water to the boil. Season 1 pan of water with salt, and drop in the tagliatelle. Cook according to the packet instructions – usually about 10–12 minutes. Drop the washed spinach into the other pan of water. As soon as the spinach has wilted, remove and cool under the cold tap. Drain and squeeze dry, then roughly chop and set aside.

2 Heat the olive oil in a sauté pan over a medium-low heat. Add the finely sliced shallots, garlic and chilli flakes and gently fry until soft. Then mix in the chopped, blanched spinach, mascarpone, lemon zest and seasoning. When piping hot, season with nutmeg and finely grated Parmesan.

3 Roughly drain the cooked pasta and toss into the sauce. Divide between 4 plates and serve with extra, finely grated, Parmesan.

bay leaf

Curiously, although bay leaves *(Laurus nobilis)* are used to enhance any intrinsic sweetness in a dish, they actually taste quite bitter. Their sweet green aroma comes from cineole, a volatile oil that gradually diminishes after the leaf is picked. Thus, they are at their most bitter-sweet when just picked. Gradually, as they dry, both their bitterness and sweet scent fades, so dried bay leaves are a mild flavouring compared to fresh.

Bay leaves can be used in both sweet and savoury dishes. Traditionally added to stocks, marinades, soups, sauces and stews, they will intensify any underlying sweetness in sour, salty, umami, bitter or sweet foods, regardless of whether it is in a wine marinade, tomato sauce or beef casserole. The bay leaf's aromatic properties also add a greater depth of sweet flavour to milk-based concoctions, from a savoury white sauce to a sweet custard.

béchamel sauce

The bay leaf enhances the sweetness of this milk sauce, while the mace adds a hint of freshness.

makes 425ml (¾ pint)

425ml (¾ pint) whole milk
1 small onion, halved
1 bay leaf
6 black peppercorns
a pinch of ground mace
2 level tablespoons or about 20g (¾oz) butter
2 level tablespoons plain flour
salt

1 Place the milk, onion, bay leaf, peppercorns and mace in a small saucepan. Set over a low heat and bring up to just below boiling point, then immediately remove from the heat; cover and leave to infuse for 30 minutes.

2 Melt the butter in a heavy-bottomed saucepan over a low heat. Stir in the flour and cook gently for 2–3 minutes to make a roux. It will turn paler as it cooks. Do not let it brown.

3 Strain the milk and, using a wooden spoon, gradually stir it in, a little at a time, until it forms a smooth sauce. Once all the milk has been incorporated into the sauce, simmer very gently for 5–7 minutes, stirring occasionally until the flour tastes cooked. Season to taste with salt and use as necessary. If you need to keep the sauce warm, cover the surface with some buttered greaseproof paper to prevent it from forming a skin.

rose water

Sweet food perfumed by a few heady drops of distilled rose petals can taste sublime. Added with the lightest of hands, rose water's intensely floral scent imbues everything it touches with a sweet aroma, despite the fact that neat rose water is bitter. Thus, a sweet-sour rhubarb cordial (see p.126) or a bitter-sweet almond and pistachio baklava will taste all the sweeter yet more ethereal if flavoured with a sprinkling of rose water. It is particularly good with sweetened cream, butter and milk. However, it is also delicious with all types of nuts and certain aromatic fruits, such as quinces, apples, pears, peaches, raspberries and strawberries.

The best rose water comes from the Middle East, so seek it out from Middle Eastern or Indian shops. While there, buy some distilled orange-flower water, which adds an equally dreamy bitter-sweet citrus floral note to food.

buttered rose water apricots

The rose water transforms the intense sweet-sour taste of apricots into a sugary, fragrant flavour. This also makes an amazing pie filling, especially if topped with equally buttery puff pastry. Simply coat the apricots in the sugary mixture, add rose water and tip into the pie dish; cover and bake as usual.

serves 4
30g (1oz) unsalted butter
140g (5oz) caster sugar
680g (1½lb) apricots, halved and stoned
1 teaspoon distilled rose water

1 Place the butter and sugar in a large non-stick frying pan and set over a low heat. Stir until the butter has melted, then mix in the halved apricots, making sure that they are well coated.

2 Keep stirring until the sugar has melted and the apricots are beginning to exude their juice. Cover and cook gently, stirring occasionally, for about 8 minutes or until the apricots are tender but not mushy. Then remove from the heat and add the rose water to taste. Serve warm with clotted cream or crème fraîche.

saffron

The fragile deep orange filaments of saffron impart bitterness to food, mixed with an intense honeyed scent and brilliant gold colour. They are the dried, hand-picked stigmas of *Crocus sativus*, an autumn-flowering violet-blue crocus widely grown in Iran, Kashmir and Spain. Over thousands of years, saffron has developed a mystique, due mainly to the expense of harvesting some 80,000 flowers to make a mere 450g (1lb) of saffron threads. Nevertheless, a small pinch will give an intriguing hint of bitterness to savoury and sweet dishes.

Saffron's bitterness resonates with the bitterness in olive oil, almonds, citrus zest and olives. It transforms the one-dimensional sweetness of rice, butter, cream and potatoes into something complex and satisfying. It draws out the intrinsic sweetness of meat, fowl and fish and creates a symphony of alluring tastes when combined in a stew with umami tomatoes, salty broth or sour citrus juice. Always buy small quantities of the best quality (usually the most expensive) saffron you can find and keep it in an airtight container in a cool, dark place.

saffron rice

The sweet-salty-umami nature of rice simmered with sautéed shallots and stock is made even more satisfying with the hint of honeyed bitterness from the saffron. As a basic rule for cooking basmati rice, always add double the volume of liquid to rice. In other words, use 1 cup of rice to 2 cups of stock for 2 people.

serves 2

a pinch of saffron threads
425ml (¾ pint) hot chicken stock
1 tablespoon olive oil
1 shallot, finely sliced
170g (6oz) basmati rice
salt

1 Grind the saffron threads under a teaspoon until they form a powder. Place in a bowl and cover with hot chicken stock; leave to infuse.

2 Heat the olive oil in a saucepan and gently fry the sliced shallot until soft. Stir in the rice and cook for a further 3 minutes, or until it looks slightly translucent.

3 Add all the tepid saffron stock, season to taste with salt, cover and increase the heat. As soon as it comes to the boil, reduce the heat to low and simmer for 15 minutes. Then turn off the heat and leave for 5 minutes. The rice is ready when it is fluffy and just past *al dente*. All the liquid should have been absorbed.

vanilla pod

The merest sniff of the fermented pod of the climbing orchid *Vanilla planifolia* suggests sweetness to the cook. It adds a luscious, aromatic sweetness to sweet dishes made with cream, butter, sugar or eggs, and softens acidity in wine or fruit such as peaches, nectarines, plums and sour cherries. Vanilla gives the illusion of sweetness in bitter chocolate, caramel or coffee puddings. There has been a fashion to use it in sweet-salty-savoury dishes, in particular by infusing vanilla into a butter sauce to serve with fish, but to my mind it is best restricted to puddings, cakes and sweetmeats.

The perfect vanilla pod should be lustrous black-brown, flecked with white crystals of vanillin dust, and supple enough to twist around your finger without rupturing. Store in an airtight jar and, once used, rinse lightly, allow to dry and slip into your caster sugar. As a second choice, you can use vanilla extract (essence) – an alcoholic infusion of finely chopped second-grade vanilla pods. Never use vanilla 'flavouring', which is made by chemically synthesizing pure vanillin from sawdust. It utterly lacks the heady complex aroma that is created by more than 70 compounds in a vanilla pod.

vanilla custard

Vanilla somehow adds a sumptuous sweet depth to a simple custard. This recipe is for cold custard, but if you wish to serve it warm, add the cream directly to the custard, allow to heat through without boiling and transfer the saucepan to a bain-marie of hot (not boiling) water or keep in a thermos flask until ready to serve.

makes 565ml (1 pint)

425ml (¾ pint) milk
1 vanilla pod, cut open lengthways
115g (4oz) caster sugar
140ml (¼ pint) double cream
6 medium egg yolks
a tiny pinch of salt

1 Place the milk, vanilla pod and half the sugar in a saucepan. Heat to just below boiling point, stirring occasionally to ensure that all the sugar dissolves. Remove from the heat, cover and leave to infuse for 30 minutes.

2 Fill a large bowl with ice and set a medium-sized bowl over it. Pour the double cream into the bowl; set aside.

3 Whisk the egg yolks with a tiny pinch of salt and the remaining sugar until they leave a trail. Gradually stir in the milk (with the vanilla pod) and immediately return the mixture to the saucepan. Still stirring with a wooden spoon, set over a low heat and continue to stir until the custard is as thick as runny double cream. Do not let the custard boil or it will split. Immediately pour into the bowl of iced cream and stir until it is tepid. Remove the vanilla pod and serve chilled.

chicken stock

This brown chicken stock has a classic umami taste which can be used to great effect in other dishes. This recipe can be adapted to make lamb stock by replacing the chicken with four raw lamb leg bones.

makes 2 litres

2 good organic or free range chickens
5 tablespoons sunflower oil
3 onions, halved
4 shallots
3 fat garlic cloves
4 large carrots, peeled and cut in half
4 outer sticks of celery, halved
3 leeks, cut into chunks
handful parsley stalks with some thyme sprigs
1 bay leaf
½ bottle white wine
6 black peppercorns
2 cloves

1 Preheat the oven to its highest setting. Remove the legs from each chicken by pulling the thigh away from the body and cutting around the thigh joint. Cut each leg in half and place in a roasting tray. Cut off the wing tips, then slice each breast away from the rib cage. Cut off the wings and wrap and chill the chicken breasts to be used for another dish. Add the wing joints to the legs. Slice off and discard the parson's nose, then cut each carcass in half by snapping through the spine. Place in the roasting tray. Toss the chicken in 2 tablespoons sunflower oil and place in the centre of the oven. Roast for about 30 minutes, or until golden brown.

2 Heat 3 tablespoons oil in a stock pot and set over a medium heat. Add the onions, shallots, garlic, carrots and celery, stirring regularly, until the vegetables are lightly coloured. Then add the leeks, herbs and wine and set aside until the chicken is ready.

3 Transfer the chicken pieces to the saucepan. Discard the fat in the roasting tray. Fill the pan with cold water, covering the chicken, and set over a high heat.

4 As the stock comes to the boil, skim off the fat and scum that form on the surface. Skim regularly until the liquid begins to boil properly, then immediately reduce the temperature to a gentle simmer and add the peppercorns and cloves.

5 Simmer gently for the next 5 hours, topping up once with enough water to cover the bones after the first 2 hours. It is ready when it tastes wonderful and has reduced by about a third to a half. Strain the liquid through a fine sieve and set aside to cool. Once cold, chill, covered in the fridge. Skim off the fat, decant into smaller containers and freeze until needed.

shortcrust pastry

Savoury pastry tastes almost sweet because butter and flour are slightly sweet. This taste can be accentuated for puddings by adding a teaspoon of icing sugar.

makes 225g (8oz) pastry

225g (8oz) plain flour
½ teaspoon salt
115g (4oz) cold butter
cold water

Quick method

1 Place the flour and salt in a food processor and give a quick whizz to mix and lighten. Cut the butter into small cubes and add to the flour. Start the processor, stopping frequently to check the consistency of the butter and flour. Stop as soon as the butter and flour have turned into fine crumbs. If you over-process they will become a paste, which will make your pastry very short.

2 Transfer the mixture to a mixing bowl and cautiously add a little cold water. Mix with a fork, adding a little more water if necessary, until the crumbs begin to form themselves into larger balls of dough. At this stage place the dough on a scantily floured surface and lightly knead by hand. Wrap in foil and refrigerate for 30 minutes. Roll when needed.

Manual method

1 Sift the flour and salt into a large mixing bowl. Cut the butter into very small dice and add. Using your fingertips, lightly rub the butter into the flour until it forms fine crumbs.

2 Add the cold water and continue as per the quick method above.

Note: it is worth making double quantities of pastry and storing in the freezer as it freezes well.

bibliography

Stephanie Alexander, *The Cook's Companion*, Viking, 1996.

Peter Barham, *The Science of Cooking*, Springer, 2000.

Jennifer Brennan, *Thai Cooking*, Jill Norman & Hobhouse, 1981.

Savitri Chowdhary, *Indian Cooking*, Pan Books, 1978.

Elizabeth David, *Spices, Salt and Aromatics in the English Kitchen*, Penguin, 1975.

Alan Davidson, *The Oxford Companion to Food*, Oxford University Press, 1999.

Dave DeWitt & Paul W. Bosland, *The Pepper Garden*, Ten Speed Press, 1993.

Fuchsia Dunlop, *Sichuan Cookery*, Michael Joseph, 2001.

Jane Grigson, *Jane Grigson's Fruit Book*, Michael Joseph, 1982.

Jane Grigson, *Jane Grigson's Vegetable Book*, Penguin, 1979.

Sybil Kapoor, *Modern British Food*, Penguin, 1996.

Sybil Kapoor, *Simply British*, Penguin, 1999.

Colonel A.R. Kenney-Herbert, *Culinary Jottings for Madras by 'Wyvern'* (1885) Prospect Books, 1994.

Larousse Gastronomique, Hamyln, 2001.

Hsian Ju Lin & Tsuifeng Lin, *Chinese Gastronomy*, Thomas Nelson and Sons, 1969.

Bernd Lindemann, 'Receptors and Transduction in Taste', *Nature*, Vol 413, 13 September 2001.

Christine Manfield, *Spice*, Viking, 1999.

Chirtine McFadden & Michael Michaud, *Cool Green Leaves & Red Hot Peppers*, Frances Lincoln, 1998.

Harold McGee, *On Food and Cooking, The Science and Lore of the Kitchen*, Unwin Hyman, 1988.

Janet Mendel, *Traditional Spanish Cooking*, Garnet Publishing, 1996.

Sri Owen, *Indonesian Food and Cookery*, Prospect Books, 1986.

Apicius Redivivus (Dr. Kitchener), *The Cook's Oracle*, John Hatchard, 1818.

Clauda Roden, *A Book of Middle Eastern Food*, Penguin, 1982.

Maxime Rodinson, A.J. Arberry & Charles Perry, *Medieval Arab Cookery*, Prospect Books, 2001.

Helen Saberi, *Noshe Djan Afghan Food & Cookery*, Prospect Books, 2000.

Margaret Shaida, *The Legendary Cuisine of Persia*, Penguin, 1994.

David V. Smith and Robert F. Margolskee, Making Sense of Taste, *Scientific American*, March 2001.

Tom Stobart, *Herbs, Spices and Flavourings (1970)*, Grub Street, 1998.

Reay Tannahill, *Food in History (1988)*, Penguin.

Shizuo Tsuji, *Japanese Cooking, A Simple Art*, Kodansha International, 1985.

J.G. Vaughan & C.A. Geissler, *The New Oxford Book of Food Plants*, Oxford University Press, 1997.

Alice Waters, *Chez Panisse Vegetables*, Harper Collins, 1996.

Paula Wolfert, *Moroccan Cuisine*, Grub Street, 1998.

conversion tables

weights

metric	imperial
7.5 g	¼ oz
15 g	½ oz
20 g	¾ oz
30 g	1 oz
35 g	1¼ oz
40 g	1½ oz
50 g	1¾ oz
55 g	2 oz
65 g	2¼ oz
70 g	2½ oz
80 g	2¾ oz
85 g	3 oz
90 g	3½ oz
115 g	4 oz
140 g	5 oz
170 g	6 oz
200 g	7 oz
225 g	8 oz
255 g	9 oz
285 g	10 oz
310 g	11 oz
340 g	12 oz
370 g	13 oz
400 g	14 oz
425 g	15 oz
450 g	1 lb
565 g	1¼ lb
680 g	1½ lb
795 g	1¾ lb 2 lb
905 g	2 lb
1 kg	2 lb 3 oz
1.1 kg	2½ lb
1.4 kg	3 lb
1.5 kg	3½ lb
1.8 kg	4 lb
2 kg	4½ lb
2.3 kg	5 lb
2.7 kg	6 lb
3.1 kg	7 lb
3.6 kg	8 lb
4.5 kg	10 lb

volume

metric	imperial	
5 ml	1 teaspoon	
10 ml	1 dessertspoon	
15 ml	0.5 fl oz	
20 ml		
25 ml		
30 ml	1 fl oz	
35 ml		
40 ml	1.5 fl oz	
45 ml		
50 ml		
55 ml	2 fl oz	
60 ml		
70 ml	2.5 fl oz	
75 ml		
80 ml		
85 ml	3 fl oz	
90 ml		
95 ml		
100 ml	3.5 fl oz	
105 ml		
115 ml	4 fl oz	
120 ml		
130 ml	4.5 fl oz	
140 ml	5 fl oz	¼ pint
155 ml	5.5 fl oz	
170 ml	6 fl oz	
180 ml		
185 ml	6.5 fl oz	
200 ml	7 fl oz	
215 ml	7.5 fl oz	
225 ml	8 fl oz	
240 ml	8.5 fl oz	
255 ml	9 fl oz	
270 ml	9.5 fl oz	
285 ml	10 fl oz	½ pint
400 ml	14 fl oz	
425 ml	15 fl oz	¾ pint
565 ml	20 fl oz	1 pint
710 ml	25 fl oz	1¼ pint
850 ml	30 fl oz	1½ pint
1 litre	35 fl oz	1¾ pint

oven temperatures

heat	metric	imperial	gas
very cool	110C	225 F	Gas ¼
very cool	130C	250 F	Gas ½
cool	140C	275 F	Gas 1
slow	150C	300 F	Gas 2
moderately slow	170C	325 F	Gas 3
moderate	180C	350 F	Gas 4
moderately hot	190C	375 F	Gas 5
hot	200C	400 F	Gas 6
very hot	220C	425 F	Gas 7
very hot	230C	450 F	Gas 8
hottest	240C	475 F	Gas 9

cook's notes

The measurements in this book are metric and imperial. Consequently, American fluid measurements will differ slightly from their British namesakes. An American pint is 16 fl oz, whereas an imperial (British) pint is 20 fl oz. Thus, an American ½ pint is 8 fl oz and an imperial ½ pint is 10 fl oz.

Australian cups and tablespoons also vary slightly from their American and British counterparts. While a teaspoon is 5ml across the world, an Australian tablespoon measures 20ml (4 teaspoons) whereas a British and American tablespoon measures 15ml (3 teaspoons).

Australian cups hold 250ml liquid (scant imperial 9 fl oz). American (and those commonly sold in Britain) hold 225ml (imperial 8 fl oz). In other words, when in doubt, stick to metric. Unless specified in the recipe, spoon and cup measurements are always level.

Lastly, a brief note on oven temperature – a constant dilemma for food writers! The oven temperatures in this book are based on my well-tempered fan-assisted oven, but you may have to adjust them slightly if you don't have a fan-assisted oven or if your oven is particularly fierce or cool.

index